ISLAM OBSERVED

Religious Development in Morocco and Indonesia

Clifford Geertz

The University of Chicago Press

Chicago & London

for Hilly

THE UNIVERSITY OF CHICAGO PRESS, CHICAGO 60637
The University of Chicago Press, Ltd., London

Copyright © 1968 by Yale University
All rights reserved
University of Chicago Press edition 1971
Printed in the United States of America

99 98 97 96 95 94 93 92 91   10 9

International Standard Book Number: 0-226-28511-1

Contents

Maps

Preface

"Bad poets borrow," T. S. Eliot has said, "good poets steal." I have tried in what follows to be, in this respect anyway, a good poet, and to take what I have needed from certain others and make it shamelessly my own. But such thievery is in great part general and undefined, an almost unconscious process of selection, absorption, and reworking, so that after awhile one no longer quite knows where one's argument comes from, how much of it is his and how much is others'. One only knows, and that incompletely, what the major intellectual influences upon his work have been, but to attach specific names to specific passages is arbitrary or libelous. Let me, then, merely record that my approach to the comparative study of religion has been shaped by my reactions, as often rejecting as accepting, to the methods and concepts of Talcott Parsons, Clyde Kluckhohn, Edward Shils, Robert Bellah, and Wilfred Cantwell Smith, and their intellectual presence can be discerned, not always in forms of which they would approve, throughout the whole of this little book, as can that of the man whose genius made both their and my work possible, Max Weber. The certification of fact is, of course, another matter: to the degree that references documentary to my substantive assertions can be given, they will be found in the bibliographical note at the end of the book.

In four brief chapters—originally delivered as the Terry Foundation Lectures on Religion and Science for 1967 at Yale University—I have attempted both to lay out a general framework for the comparative analysis of religion and to apply it to a study of the development of a supposedly single creed, Islam, in two quite contrasting civilizations, the Indonesian and the Moroccan. Merely to state such a program is to demonstrate a certain lack of grasp upon reality. What results can only be too abbreviated to be balanced and too speculative to be demonstrable. Two cultures over two thousand years are hardly to be compressed into forty thousand words, and to hope, besides, to interpret the course of their spiritual life in terms of some general considerations is to court superficiality and confusion at the same time.

Yet there is something to be said for sketches as for oils and at the present stage of scholarship on Indonesian and Moroccan Islam (to say nothing of comparative religion, which as a scientific discipline hardly more than merely exists), sketches may be all that can be expected. For my part, I have drawn the inspiration, if that is the word for it, for my sketch mainly out of my own fieldwork as an anthropologist in the two countries concerned. In 1952–54, I spent two years in Java studying the religious and social life of a small town in the east-central part of the island, as well as pursuing various topics in Djakarta and Jogjakarta. In 1957–58, I was back in Indonesia, concentrating my efforts on Bali, but spending some time in Sumatra, and, once again, Central Java, as well. In 1964 and again in 1965–66, I conducted similar researches (which are, as a matter of fact, still in progress) in Morocco, working mainly in a small, ancient walled city in the interior, but there, too, journeying about the country generally. An anthropologist's work tends, no matter what its ostensible subject, to be but an expression of his research experience, or, more accurately, of what his research experience has done to him. Certainly this has been true for me. Fieldwork has been, for me, intellectually (and not only intellectually) formative, the source not just of discrete hypotheses but of whole patterns of social and cultural interpretation. The bulk of what I have eventually seen (or thought I have seen) in the broad sweep of social history I have seen (or thought I have seen) first in the narrow confines of country towns and peasant villages.

A number of people—historians mostly, but political scientists, sociologists, and economists as well—have questioned whether this sort of procedure is a defensible one. Is it not invalid to read off the contours of a whole civilization, a national economy, an encompassing political system, a pervasive class structure, from the details of some miniature social system, however intimately known? Is it not reckless to assume any such miniature social system—some bypath town or village or region—is typical of the country as a whole? Is it not absurd to divine the shape of the past in a limited body of data drawn from the present? The answer to all these questions, and others like them, is, of course, "yes": it is invalid, reckless, absurd—and impossible. But the questions are misplaced. Anthropologists are not (or, to be more candid, not any longer) attempting to substitute parochial understandings for comprehensive ones, to reduce America to Jonesville or Mexico to Yucatan. They are attempting (or, to be more precise, I am attempting) to discover what contributions parochial understandings can make to comprehensive ones, what leads to general, broad-stroke interpretations particular, intimate findings can produce. I myself cannot see how this differs, save in content, from what an historian, political scientist, sociologist, or economist does, at least when he turns away from his own versions of Jonesville and Yucatan and addresses himself to wider problems. We are all special scientists now, and our worth, at least in this regard, consists of what we are able to contribute to a task, the understanding of human social life, which no one of us is competent to tackle unassisted.

The fact that the anthropologist's insights, such as they are, grow (in part) out of his intensive fieldwork in particular settings does not, then, in itself invalidate them. But if such insights are to apply to anything beyond those settings, if they are to transcend their parochial origins and achieve a more cosmopolitan relevance, they quite obviously cannot also be validated there. Like all scientific propositions, anthropological interpretations must be tested against the material they are designed to interpret; it is not their origins that recommend them. For someone who spends the overwhelming proportion of the research phases of his scholarly life wandering about rice terraces or blacksmith shops talking to this farmer and that artisan in what he takes to be the latter's vernacular, the realization of this fact can be a shaking experience. One can cope with it either by confining oneself to one's chosen stage and letting others make of one's descriptions what they will (in which case the generalization of them is likely to be even more uncritical and uncontrolled), or one can take up, in the absence of any particular competence to do so, the task of demonstrating that less special sorts of material and less minutely focused problems can be made to yield to the same kinds of analysis practiced on the narrowed scene. To choose the second alternative is to commit oneself to facing up to the necessity of subjecting one's theories and observations to tests quite unlike those to which anthropological arguments are normally required to submit. What was private domain, neatly fenced and intimately known, becomes foreign ground, heavily traversed but personally unfamiliar.

In these lectures I have, as I have already indicated, followed the second course with something of a vengeance. In doing so, I have sought to see what sense I could make of the religious histories of Morocco and Indonesia in terms both of what I have concluded from my field studies and what, in more general terms, I think religion comes down to as a social, cultural, and psychological phenomenon. But the validity of both my empirical conclusions and my theoretical premises rests, in the end, on how effective they are in so making sense of data from which they were neither derived nor for which they were originally designed. The test of their worth lies there, as comparative, historical, macrosociology. A half-century after Weber's death, this sociology is still very largely a program. But it is a program, I think, well worth attempting to effect. For without it we are prey, on the one hand, to the pallid mindlessness of radical relativism and, on the other, to the shabby tyranny of historical determinism.

Lloyd Fallers, Hildred Geertz, Lawrence Rosen, David Schneider, and Melford Spiro have all given earlier drafts of this work the benefit of extensive and careful criticism, some of which I have paid attention to. I am grateful to them.

C. G.

Chicago
January 1968

1. Two Countries, Two Cultures

Of all the dimensions of the uncertain revolution now underway in the new states of Asia and Africa, surely the most difficult to grasp is the religious. It is not measurable as, however inexactly, economic change is. It is not, for the most part, illuminated by the instructive explosions that mark political development: purges, assassinations, coups d'etat, border wars, riots, and here and there an election. Such proven indices of mutation in the forms of social life as urbanization, the solidification of class loyalties, or the growth of a more complex occupational system are, if not wholly lacking, certainly rarer and a great deal more equivocal in the religious sphere, where old wine goes as easily into new bottles as old bottles contain new wine. It is not only very difficult to discover the ways in which the shapes of religious experience are changing, or if they are changing at all; it is not even clear what sorts of things one ought to look at in order to find out.

The comparative study of religion has always been plagued by this peculiar embarrassment: the elusiveness of its subject matter. The problem is not one of constructing definitions of religion. We have had quite enough of those; their very number is a symptom of our malaise. It is a matter of discovering just what sorts of beliefs and practices support what sorts of faith under what sorts of conditions. Our problem, and it grows worse by the day, is not to define religion but to find it.

This may seem an odd thing to say. What is in those thick volumes on totemic myths, initiation rites, witchcraft beliefs, shamanistic performances, and so on, which ethnographers have been compiling with such astonishing industry for over a century? Or in the equally thick and not much more readable works by historians on the development of Judaic law, Confucian philosophy, or Christian theology? Or in the countless sociological studies of such institutions as Indian caste or Islamic sectarianism, Japanese emperor worship or African cattle sacrifice? Do they not contain our subject matter? The answer is, quite simply, no: they contain the record of our search for our subject matter. The search has not been without its successes, and our appointed task is to keep it going and enlarge its successes. But the aim of the systematic study of religion is, or anyway ought to be, not just to describe ideas, acts, and institutions, but to determine just how and in what way particular ideas, acts, and institutions sustain, fail to sustain, or even inhibit religious faith—that is to say, steadfast attachment to some transtemporal conception of reality.

There is nothing mysterious in this, nor anything doctrinal. It merely means that we must distinguish between a religious attitude toward experience and the sorts of social apparatus which have, over time and space, customarily been associated with supporting such an attitude. When this is done, the comparative study of religion shifts from a kind of advanced curio collecting to a kind of not very advanced science; from a discipline in which one merely records, classifies, and perhaps even generalizes about data deemed, plausibly enough in most cases, to have something to do with religion to one in which one asks close questions of such data, not the least important of which is just what does it have to do with religion. We can scarcely hope to get far with the analysis of religious change—that is to say, what happens to faith when its vehicles alter—if we are unclear as to what in any particular case its vehicles are and how (or even *if*) in fact they foster it.

Whatever the ultimate sources of the faith of a man or group of men may or may not be, it is indisputable that it is sustained in this world by symbolic forms and social arrangements. What a given religion is—its specific content—is embodied in the images and metaphors its adherents use to characterize reality; it makes, as Kenneth Burke once pointed out, a great deal of difference whether you call life a dream, a pilgrimage, a labyrinth, or a carnival. But such a religion's career—its historical course—rests in turn upon the institutions which render these images and metaphors available to those who thus employ them. It is really not much easier to conceive of Christianity without Gregory than without Jesus. Or if that remark seems tendentious (which it is not), then Islam without the Ulema than without Muhammad; Hinduism without caste than without the Vedas; Confucianism without the mandarinate than without the Analects; Navaho religion without Beauty Way than without Spider Woman. Religion may be a stone thrown into the world; but it must be a palpable stone and someone must throw it.

If this is accepted (and if it is not accepted the result is to remove religion not merely from scholarly examination and rational discourse, but from life altogether), then even a cursory glance at the religious situation in the new states collectively or in any one of them separately will reveal the major direction of change: established connections between particular varieties of faith and the cluster of images and institutions which have classically nourished them are for certain people in certain circumstances coming unstuck. In the new states as in the old, the intriguing question for the anthropologist is, "How do men of religious sensibility react when the machinery of faith begins to wear out? What do they do when traditions falter?"

They do, of course, all sorts of things. They lose their sensibility. Or they channel it into ideological fervor. Or they adopt an imported creed. Or they turn worriedly in upon themselves. Or they cling even more intensely to the faltering traditions. Or they try to rework those traditions into more effective forms. Or they split themselves in half, living spiritually in the past and physically in the present. Or they try to express their religiousness in secular activities. And a few simply fail to notice their world is moving or, noticing, just collapse.

But such general answers are not really very enlightening, not only because they are general but because they glide past that which we most want to know: by what means, what social and cultural processes, are these movements toward skepticism, political enthusiasm, conversion, revivalism, subjectivism, secular piety, reformism, double-mindedness, or whatever, taking place? What new forms of architecture are housing these accumulating changes of heart?

In attempting to answer grand questions like this, the anthropologist is always inclined to turn toward the concrete, the particular, the microscopic. We are the miniaturists of the social sciences, painting on lilliputian canvases with what we take to be delicate strokes. We hope to find in the little what eludes us in the large, to stumble upon general truths while sorting through special cases. At least I hope to, and in that spirit I want to discuss religious change in the two countries in which I have worked at some length, Indonesia and Morocco. They make from some points of view an odd pair: a rarefied, somewhat overcivilized tropical Asian country speckled with Dutch culture, and a taut, arid, rather puritanical Mediterranean one varnished with French. But from some other points of view—including the fact that they are both in some enlarged sense of the word Islamic—they make an instructive comparison. At once very alike and very different, they form a kind of commentary on one another's character.

Their most obvious likeness is, as I say, their religious affiliation; but it is also, culturally speaking at least, their most obvious unlikeness. They stand at the eastern and western extremities of the narrow band of classical Islamic civilization which, rising in Arabia, reached out along the midline of the Old World to connect them, and, so located, they have participated in the history of that civilization in quite different ways, to quite different degrees, and with quite different results. They both incline toward Mecca, but, the antipodes of the Muslim world, they bow in opposite directions.

As a Muslim country, Morocco is of course the older. The first contact with Islam—a military one, as the Ummayads made their brief bid for sovereignty over Alexander's "all the inhabited world"—came in the seventh century, only fifty years after the death of Muhammed; and by the middle of the eighth century a solid, if not exactly indestructible, Muslim foothold had been established. Over the next three centuries it was rendered indestructible, and the great age of Berber Islam, the one which Ibn Khaldun looked back upon with such a modern blend of cultural admiration and sociological despair, began. One after the other, the famous reforming dynasties—Almoravids, Almohads, Merinids —swept out of what the French, with fine colonial candor, used to call *le Maroc inutile*, the forts and oases of the pre-Sahara, the walled-in rivers and pocket plateaus of the High Atlas, and the wastes of the Algerian steppe, into *le Maroc utile*, the mild and watered Cis-Atlas plains. Building and rebuilding the great cities of Morocco—Marrakech, Fez, Rabat, Salé, Tetuan—they penetrated Muslim Spain, absorbed its culture and, reworking it into their own more strenuous ethos, reproduced a simplified version of it on their side of Gibraltar. The formative period both of Morocco as a nation and of Islam as its creed (roughly 1050 to 1450) consisted of the peculiar process of tribal edges falling in upon an agricultural center and civilizing it. It was the periphery of the country, the harsh and sterile frontiers, that nourished and in fact created the advanced society which developed at its heart.

As time went on, the contrast between the artisans, notables, scholars, and shopkeepers assembled within the walls of the great cities and the farmers and pastoralists scattered thinly over the countryside around them naturally widened. The former developed a sedentary society centered on trade and craft, the latter a mobile one centered on herding and tillage. Yet the difference between the two was far from absolute; townsman and countryman did not live in different cultural worlds but, a few withdrawn highland groups perhaps aside, in the same one differently situated. Rural and urban society were variant states of a single system (and there were, in fact, a half-dozen versions of each). Far from unaffecting one another, their interaction, though often antagonistic, was continuous and intense and provided the central

dynamic of historical change in Morocco from the founding of Fez at the beginning of the ninth century to its occupation by the French at the beginning of the twentieth.

There were several reasons for this. The first is that, as mentioned, the towns were at base tribal creations and, transient moments of introversion aside, largely remained so. Each major phase of civilization (and indeed most minor ones as well) began with a breaching of the gates by some ambitious local chieftain whose religious zeal was the source of both his ambition and his chieftainship.

Second, the combination of the intrusion into the western plains after the thirteenth century of marauding Bedouin Arabs, and the fact that Morocco is located not at the core of the grain-growing world but at its furthest frontiers, prevented the development of a mature peasant culture which would have buffered tribesmen from townsmen and allowed them, milking the peasantry of tribute or taxes, to go more independently along their separate ways. As it was, neither urban nor rural life was ever altogether viable. The cities, under the leadership of their viziers and sultans, tried always to reach out around them to control the tribes. But the latter remained footloose and refractory, as well as unrewarding. The uncertainty of both pastoralism and agriculture in this climatically irregular, physically ill-endowed, and somewhat despoiled environment impelled tribesmen sometimes into the cities, if not as conquerors then as refugees, sometimes out of their reach in mountain passes or desert wastes, and sometimes toward encircling them and, blocking the trade routes from which they lived, extorting from them. The political metabolism of traditional Morocco consisted of two but intermittently workable economies attempting, according to season and circumstance, to feed off one another.

And third, the cities were not crystal islands set in a shapeless sea. The fluidity of town life was hardly less than that of rural, just somewhat more confined, while the forms of tribal society were as clearly outlined as those of metropolitan. In fact, adjusted to different environments, they were the same forms, animated by the same ideals. What varied in traditional Morocco was less the kind of life different groups of people attempted to live than the ecological niches in which they attempted to live it.

Andalusian decorations, Berber folkways, and Arabian state-craft to the contrary notwithstanding, therefore, the basic style of life in, to use another term from the pointed rhetoric of the Protec-torate, *le Maroc disparu*, was about everywhere the same: strenu-ous, fluid, violent, visionary, devout, and unsentimental, but above all, self-assertive. It was a society in which a very great deal turned on force of character and most of the rest on spiritual reputation. In town and out, its leitmotivs were strong-man politics and holy-man piety, and its fulfillments, small and large, tribal and dynas-tic, occurred when, in the person of a particular individual, they momentarily fused. The axial figure, whether he was storming walls or building them, was the warrior saint.

This is particularly apparent at the great transitional points of Moroccan history, the recurring changes of political direction in which its social identity was forged. Idris II, the ninth-century builder of Fez and the country's first substantial king, was at once a descendant of the Prophet, a vigorous military leader, and a dedicated religious purifier and would not have amounted to much as any one of these had he not concurrently been the other two. Both the Almoravid and Almohad movements were founded —the first around the middle of the eleventh century, the sec-ond toward the middle of the twelfth—by visionary reformers returning from the Middle East determined not just to inveigh against error but to dismember its carriers. The exhaustion, in the fifteenth century, of the revolution they began, and the collapse of the political order that revolution had created, was followed in turn by what was probably the greatest spiritual dislocation the country has ever experienced: the so-called Maraboutic Crisis. Lo-cal holy men, or marabouts—descendants of the Prophet, leaders of Sufi brotherhoods, or simply vivid individuals who had con-trived to make something uncanny happen—appeared all over the landscape to launch private bids for power. The period of the-ocratic anarchy and sectarian enthusiasm thus inaugurated was arrested only two centuries later (and then only very partially) with the rise, under yet one more reform-bent descendant of Muhammad, of the still reigning Alawite dynasty. And finally, when after 1911 the French and Spanish moved in to take direct control of the country, it was a series of such martial marabouts, scattered along the edges of the crumbling kingdom, who rallied the population, or parts of it, for the last brave, desperate attempt to revive the old order, the Morocco that had, in the course of the previous half-century, begun slowly but inexorably to disappear.

In any case, the critical feature of that Morocco so far as we are concerned is that its cultural center of gravity lay not, paradoxical as this may seem, in the great cities, but in the mobile, aggressive, now federated, now fragmented tribes who not only harassed and exploited them but also shaped their growth. It is out of the tribes that the forming impulses of Islamic civilization in Morocco came, and the stamp of their mentality remained on it, whatever Arabo-Spanish sophistications urban religious scholars, locking themselves away from the local current, were able, in a few selected corners and for a few chromatic moments, to introduce. Islam in Barbary was—and to a fair extent still is— basically the Islam of saint worship and moral severity, magical power and aggressive piety, and this was for all practical purposes as true in the alleys of Fez and Marrakech as in the expanses of the Atlas or the Sahara.

Indonesia is, as I say, another matter altogether. Rather than tribal it is, and for the whole of the Christian era has been, basically a peasant society, particularly in its overpowering heartland, Java. Intensive, extremely productive wet rice cultivation has provided the main economic foundations of its culture for about as long as we have record, and rather than the restless, aggressive, extroverted sheikh husbanding his resources, cultivating his reputation, and awaiting his opportunity, the national archetype is the

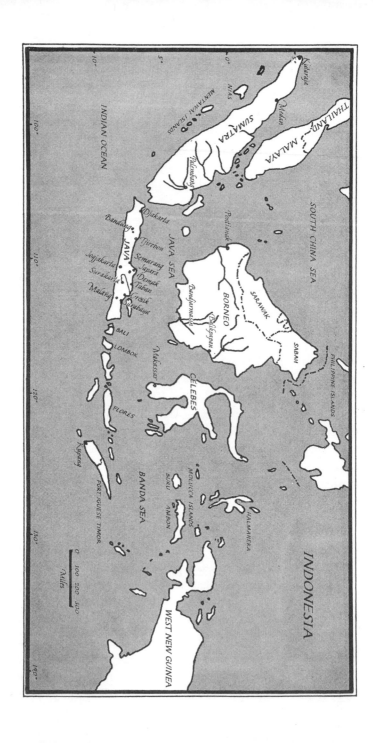

settled, industrious, rather inward plowman of twenty centuries, nursing his terrace, placating his neighbors, and feeding his superiors. In Morocco civilization was built on nerve; in Indonesia, on diligence.

Further, not only was classical Indonesian civilization founded upon the rock of a spectacularly productive peasant economy, but it was not in the first instance Islamic at all, but Indic. Unlike the way it moved into Morocco, Islam—which arrived with genuine definitiveness only after the fourteenth century—did not, except for a few pockets in Sumatra, Borneo, and the Celebes, move into an essentially virgin area, so far as high culture was concerned, but into one of Asia's greatest political, aesthetic, religious, and social creations, the Hindu-Buddhist Javanese state, which though it had by then begun to weaken, had cast its roots so deeply into Indonesian society (especially on Java, but not only there) that its impress remained proof not just to Islamization, but to Dutch imperialism and, so far anyway, to modern nationalism as well. It is perhaps as true for civilizations as it is for men that, however much they may later change, the fundamental dimensions of their character, the structure of possibilities within which they will in some sense always move, are set in the plastic period when they first are forming. In Morocco, this period was the age of the Berber dynasties, which, whatever their local peculiarities, were at least generally driven by Islamic ideals and concepts. In Indonesia, it was the age (roughly contemporaneous, actually) of the great Indic states—Mataram, Singosari, Kediri, Madjapahit—which, though also importantly shaped by local traditions, were generally guided by Indic theories of cosmic truth and metaphysical virtue. In Indonesia Islam did not construct a civilization, it appropriated one.

These two facts, that the main impulse for the development of a more complex culture—true state organization, long-distance trade, sophisticated art, and universalistic religion—grew out of a centrally located peasant society upon which less developed outlying regions pivoted, rather than the other way around, and that Islam penetrated this axial culture well after it had been securely established, account for the overall cast Muhammedanism has taken in Indonesia. Compared to North Africa, the Middle East, and even to Muslim India, whose brand of faith it perhaps most closely resembles, Indonesian Islam has been, at least until recently, remarkably malleable, tentative, syncretistic, and, most significantly of all, multivoiced. What for so many parts of the world, and certainly for Morocco, has been a powerful, if not always triumphant, force for cultural homogenization and moral consensus, for the social standardization of fundamental beliefs and values, has been for Indonesia a no less powerful one for cultural diversification, for the crystalization of sharply variant, even incompatible, notions of what the world is really like and how one ought therefore to set about living in it. In Indonesia Islam has taken many forms, not all of them Koranic, and whatever it brought to the sprawling archipelago, it was not uniformity.

Islam came, in any case, by sea and on the heels not of conquest but of trade. Its initial triumphs were consequently along the coastal areas rimming the tranquil Java Sea and its approaches— the bustling ports, merchant princedoms actually, of northern Sumatra, southwest Malaya, south Borneo, south Celebes, and, most important of all, north Java. In the non-Javanese areas the new faith (new in form anyway; as it had come to the island not out of Arabia but India, it was not quite so new in substance) remained largely confined to the coastal areas, to the harbor towns and their immediate environs. But on Java, where the cultural center of gravity was inland in the great volcanic rise basins and where European presence along the coast soon became the commanding force, it had a rather different career. In the Outer Island enclaves it remained, or at least developed into, the sort of exclusivistic, undecorated, and emphatic creed we associate with the main line of Muslim tradition, though even there the entanglement with Indian pantheism, in both the archipelago and the subcontinent, gave it a perceptibly theosophical tinge. In Java, however—where, in the end, the overwhelming majority of Indonesian Muslims were to be found—the tinge became at once a great deal deeper and much less evenly suffused.

As the Dutch closed in upon Java from the seventeenth to the nineteenth centuries, a rather curious process of cultural and religious diversification took place under the general cover of overall Islamization. The indigenous trading classes, among whom Islam had taken its firmest hold, were driven away from international commerce toward domestic peddling, and thus away from the sea toward the interior; the highly Indicized native ruling classes were reduced to the status of civil servants, administering Dutch policies at the local level; the peasantry, drawn more and more into the orbit of a colonial export economy, folded back upon itself in a paroxysm of defensive solidarity. And each of these major groups absorbed the Islamic impulse in quite different ways.

The gentry, deprived of Indic ritualism but not of Indic pantheism, became increasingly subjectivist, cultivating an essentially illuminationist approach to the divine, a kind of Far Eastern gnosticism, complete with cabalistic speculations and metapsychic exercises. The peasantry absorbed Islamic concepts and practices, so far as it understood them, into the same general Southeast Asian folk religion into which it had previously absorbed Indian ones, locking ghosts, gods, jinns, and prophets together into a strikingly contemplative, even philosophical, animism. And the trading classes, relying more and more heavily upon the Meccan pilgrimage as their lifeline to the wider Islamic world, developed a compromise between what flowed into them along this line (and from their plainer colleagues in the Outer Islands) and what they confronted in Java to produce a religious system not quite doctrinal enough to be Middle Eastern and not quite ethereal enough to be South Asian. The overall result is what can properly be called syncretism, but it was a syncretism the order of whose elements, the weight and meaning given to its various ingredients, differed markedly, and what is more important, increasingly, from one sector of the society to another.

In short, to say that Morocco and Indonesia are both Islamic societies, in the sense that most everyone in them (well over nine-tenths of the population in either case) professes to be a Muslim, is as much to point up their differences as it is to locate their similarities. Religious faith, even when it is fed from a common source, is as much a particularizing force as a generalizing one, and indeed whatever universality a given religious tradition manages to attain arises from its ability to engage a widening set of individual, even idiosyncratic, conceptions of life and yet somehow sustain and elaborate them all. When it succeeds in this, the result may indeed as often be the distortion of these personal visions as their enrichment, but in any case, whether deforming private faiths or perfecting them, the tradition usually prospers. When it fails, however, to come genuinely to grips with them at all, it either hardens into scholasticism, evaporates into idealism, or fades into eclecticism; that is to say, it ceases, except as a fossil, a shadow, or a shell, really to exist. The central paradox of religious development is that, because of the progressively wider range of spiritual experience with which it is forced to deal, the further it proceeds, the more precarious it gets. Its successes generate its frustrations.

Surely this has been the case for Islam in Morocco and Indonesia. And this is true whether one talks about that largely spontaneous, for the most part slower moving, spiritual evolution which took place from the implantation of the creed to somewhere around the beginning of this century or the end of the last, or about the painfully self-conscious questionings which, with accelerating speed and rising insistency, have been accumulating since that time. In both societies, despite the radical differences in the actual historical course and ultimate (that is, contemporary) outcome of their religious development, Islamization has been a two-sided process. On the one hand, it has consisted of an effort to adapt a universal, in theory standardized and essentially unchangeable, and unusually well-integrated system of ritual and belief to the realities of local, even individual, moral and metaphysical perception. On the other, it has consisted of a struggle to maintain, in the face of this adaptive flexibility, the identity of Islam not just as religion in general but as the particular directives communicated by God to mankind through the preemptory prophecies of Muhammad.

It is the tension between these two necessities, growing progressively greater as, first gradually and then explosively, the way men and groups of men saw life and assessed it became more and more various and incommensurable under the impress of dissimilar historical experiences, growing social complexity, and heightened self-awareness, that has been the dynamic behind the expansion of Islam in both countries. But it is this tension, too, that has brought Islam in both countries to what may, without any concession to the apocalyptic temper of our time, legitimately be called a crisis. In Indonesia as in Morocco, the collision between what the Koran reveals, or what Sunni (that is, orthodox) tradition has come to regard it as revealing, and what men who call themselves Muslims actually believe is becoming more and more inescapable. This is not so much because the gap between the two is greater. It has always been very great, and I should not like to have to argue that the Javanese peasant or Berber shepherd of 1700 was any closer to the Islam of Ash-Shafi'i or Al-Ghazali than are the Westernized youth of today's Djakarta or Rabat. It is because, given the increasing diversification of individual experience, the dazzling multiformity which is the hallmark of modern consciousness, the task of Islam (and indeed of any religious tradition) to inform the faith of particular men and to be informed by it is becoming ever more difficult. A religion which would be catholic these days has an extraordinary variety of mentalities to be catholic about; and the question, can it do this and still remain a specific and persuasive force with a shape and identity of its own, has a steadily more problematical ring.

The overall strategies evolved in Morocco and in Indonesia during the premodern period for coping with this central dilemma —how to bring exotic minds into the Islamic community without betraying the vision that created it—were, as I have indicated, strikingly different, indeed almost diametrical opposites, with the result that the shapes of the religious crises which their populations now face are to a certain extent mirror images of one another.

In Morocco the approach developed was one of uncompromising rigorism. Aggressive fundamentalism, an active attempt to impress a seamless orthodoxy on the entire population, became, not without struggle, the central theme. This is not to say that the effort has been uniformly successful, or that the concept of orthodoxy that emerged was one that the rest of the Islamic world would necessarily recognize as such. But, distinctive and perhaps even errant as it was, Moroccan Islamism came over the centuries to embody a marked strain of religious and moral perfectionism, a persisting determination to establish a purified, canonical, and completely uniform creed in this, on the face of it, unpromising setting.

The Indonesian (and especially the Javanese) mode of attack was, as I say, quite the contrary: adaptive, absorbent, pragmatic, and gradualistic, a matter of partial compromises, half-way covenants, and outright evasions. The Islamism which resulted did not even pretend to purity, it pretended to comprehensiveness; not to an intensity but to a largeness of spirit. Here, too, one ought not to take the aim for the achievement, nor to deny the presence of unconformable cases. But that over its general course Islam in Indonesia has been as Fabian in spirit as in Moroccan it has been Utopian is beyond much doubt. It is also beyond much doubt that, whatever they may originally have had to recommend them, neither of these strategies, the prudential or the headlong, is any longer working very well, and the Islamization of both countries is consequently in some danger not only of ceasing to advance but in fact of beginning to recede.

As far as religion is concerned, therefore, the tale of these two peoples is essentially the story of how they have arrived, or more accurately are in the process of arriving, at obverse forms of the same predicament. But, in some contrast to the way in which spiritual confusion is usually conceived in the West, this predicament is less a matter of what to believe as of how to believe it. Viewed as a social, cultural, and psychological (that is to say, a human) phenomenon, religiousness is not merely knowing the truth, or what is taken to be the truth, but embodying it, living it, giving oneself unconditionally to it.

In the course of their separate social histories, the Moroccans and the Indonesians created, partly out of Islamic traditions, partly out of others, images of ultimate reality in terms of which they both saw life and sought to live it. Like all religious conceptions, these images carried within them their own justification; the symbols (rites, legends, doctrines, objects, events) through which they were expressed were, for those responsive to them, intrinsically coercive, immediately persuasive—they glowed with their own authority. It is this quality that they seem gradually to be losing, at least for a small but growing minority. What is believed to be true has not changed for these people, or not changed very much. What has changed is the way in which it is believed. Where there once was faith, there now are reasons, and not very convincing ones; what once were deliverances are now hypotheses, and rather strained ones. There is not much outright skepticism around, or even much conscious hypocrisy, but there is a good deal of solemn self-deception.

In Morocco this most frequently appears as a simple disjunction between the forms of religious life, particularly the more properly Islamic ones, and the substance of everyday life. Devoutness takes the form of an almost deliberate segregation of what one learns from experience and what one receives from tradition, so that perplexity is kept at bay and doctrine kept intact by not confronting the map with the landscape it is supposed to illuminate—Utopia is preserved by rendering it even more utopian. In Indonesia it most frequently appears as a proliferation of abstractions so generalized, symbols so allusive, and doctrines so programmatic that they can be made to fit any form of experience at all. The eloquence of felt particulars is smothered in a blanket of vacant theories which, touching everything, grasp nothing—Fabianism ends in elevated vagueness. But, formalism or intellectualism, it really comes down to about the same thing: holding religious views rather than being held by them.

All this is, however, still but a crumbling at the edges; the cores of both populations still cling to the classical symbols and find them compelling. Or anyway largely so; the mere awareness on the part of those for whom the inherited machinery of faith still works passably well (which is probably the most it has ever done) that it does not work nearly so well for a growing number of others casts a certain shadow over the finality of their own perceptions. Even more important, those for whom the grasping power of the classical symbols has weakened have, with only scattered exceptions, not become impervious to that power altogether, so that rather than opting for an internal or an external approach to believing they fluctuate uncertainly and irregularly between them, seeing the symbols now as emanations of the sacred, now as representations of it. A few untroubled traditionalists at one pole and even fewer radical secularists at the other aside, most Moroccans and Indonesians alternate between religiousness and what we might call religious-mindedness with such a variety of speeds and in such a variety of ways that it is very difficult in any particular case to tell where the one leaves off and the other begins. In this, as in so many things, they are, like most of the peoples of the Third World, like indeed most of those of the First and Second, rather thoroughly mixed up. As time goes on, the number of people who desire to believe, or anyway feel they somehow ought to, decreases much less rapidly than the number who are, in a properly religious sense, able to. And in this rather demographic-looking fact lies the interest of religion for those of us who would like to uncover the dynamics and determine the directions of social change in the new states of Asia and Africa.

Alterations in the general complexion of spiritual life, in the character of religious sensibility, are more than just intellectual reorientations or shifts in emotional climate, bodiless changes of the mind. They are also, and more fundamentally, social processes, transformations in the quality of collective life. Neither thought nor feeling is, at least among humans, autonomous, a self-contained stream of subjectivity, but each is inescapably dependent upon the utilization by individuals of socially available "systems of significance," cultural constructs embodied in language, custom, art, and technology—that is to say, symbols. This is as true for religiousness as it is for any other human capacity. Without collectively evolved, socially transmitted, and culturally objectified patterns of meaning—myths, rites, doctrines, fetishes, or whatever—it would not exist. And when these patterns alter, as, given the impermanence of terrestrial things, they inevitably and indeed continuously do, it alters with them. As life moves, persuasion moves with it and indeed helps to move it. More bluntly, whatever God may or may not be—living, dead, or merely ailing—religion is a social institution, worship a social activity, and faith a social force. To trace the pattern of their changes is neither to collect relics of revelation nor to assemble a chronicle of error. It is to write a social history of the imagination.

It is this sort of history, condensed and generalized, that I am going to sketch for Morocco and Indonesia in the next two chapters and then use, in the final one, as the basis for some even less circumstantial comments on the role of religion in society generally.

In the next chapter, I will trace the development and characterize the nature of what we may call, to have a name for them, the classical religious styles in Morocco and Indonesia. As these styles were, like any styles, not born adult but evolved out of others, I shall not produce a timeless snapshot of something called "traditional religion" which, as the Moroccan idiom has it, "just came and was," but attempt to show how, gradually, variously, and with more than one detour and one delay, characteristic conceptions of the nature of the divine and the way in which men should approach it became reasonably well established in each of these countries.

To accomplish this it is necessary to do several things. First, the mere story of what came after what and when must be at least generally outlined; without sequence, descriptions of the past are catalogs or fairy tales. Second, the major conceptual themes which were in this way produced must be isolated and related to one another, and their symbolic embodiments, the cultural vehicles of their expression, must be described with some specificity, so that ideas are not left floating in some shadow world of Platonic objects but have a local habitation and a name. Finally, and perhaps most important of all, the sort of social order in which such ideas could and did seem to almost everybody to be not merely appropriate but inevitable, not commendable opinions about an unknown reality which it was comforting or prudential or honorable to hold, but authentic apprehensions of a known one which it was impossible to deny, must be depicted and analyzed. If Durkheim's famous statement that God is the symbol of society is incorrect, as I think it is, it remains true that particular kinds of faith (as well as particular kinds of doubt) flourish in particular kinds of societies, and the contribution of the comparative sociology of religion to the general understanding of the spiritual dimensions of human existence both begins and ends in an uncovering of the nature of these empirical, that is to say lawful, interconnections. The material reasons why Moroccan Islam became activist, rigorous, dogmatic and more than a little anthropolatrous and why Indonesian Islam became syncretistic, reflective, multifarious, and strikingly phenomenological lie, in part anyway, in the sort of collective life within which and along with which they evolved.

The fundamental alterations in this collective life over the past seventy-five or a hundred years, the movement toward what we vaguely and somewhat equivocally call modernism, in turn implied similar alterations in these classical religious styles, and it is to this—the interaction between religious and social change—that I will devote my third chapter.

The moving force of this still far from completed social and cultural metamorphosis is usually considered to be Western impact, the shaking of the foundations of traditional culture in Asia and Africa by the dynamism of industrial Europe. This is, of course, not wrong; but the energy of this external stimulus was converted, not just in Indonesia and Morocco but everywhere that it has been felt, into internal changes: changes in the forms of economic activity, in political organization, in the bases of social stratification, in moral values and ideologies, in family life and education, and, perhaps most critically, changes in the sense of life's possibilities, in notions of what one might hope for, work for, or even expect in the world. It is these internal changes, not, at least for the most part, European culture as such, to which religious change has been on the one hand a response and on the other an incitement. Only a tiny minority in either society has had any really intimate contact with European civilization, and most of that is either very distorted, very recent, or both. What most people have had contact with is the transformations that civilization's activities induced in their own. Whatever its outside provocations, and whatever foreign borrowing may be involved, modernity, like capital, is largely made at home.

The religious crisis in Morocco and Indonesia has been and is being generated in the internal confrontation of established forms of faith with altered conditions of life, and it is out of that confrontation that the resolution of that crisis, if there is to be a resolution, will have to come. If the term "modernization" is to be given any substantial meaning and its spiritual implications uncovered, the connections between changes in the classical religious styles and such developments as rationalized forms of economic organization, the growth of political parties, labor unions, youth groups, and other voluntary associations, revised relations between the sexes, the appearance of mass communications, the emergence of new classes, and a whole host of other social novelties must be discovered.

All this is, of course, generally known. What is not known, or anyway not very well known, are the particulars of the situation, and it is only through knowing the particulars that we can advance beyond the easy banalities of common sense. Blake's remark that there is no such thing as general knowledge, that all knowledge is knowledge of particulars, may be an exaggeration. But it is no exaggeration to say, at least so far as the sociology of religion is concerned, that there is no route to general knowledge save through a dense thicket of particulars. I shall try to keep the thicket as trimmed and well weeded as I can and to avoid telling you more about Indonesian shadow plays or Moroccan saint festivals than you care to know. Nor can I, in such a compass, discuss the nonreligious changes in any fine detail. But there is, in this area, no ascent to truth without descent to cases.

In the final chapter, at any rate, I will try to make something rather more broadly relevant out of all this closet-history and micro-sociology. Anthropology is, actually, a sly and deceptive science. At the moment when it seems most deliberately removed from our own lives, it is most immediate, when it seems most insistently to be talking about the distant, the strange, the long ago, or the idiosyncratic, it is in fact talking also about the close, the familiar, the contemporary, and the generic. From one point of view, the whole history of the comparative study of religion from the time Robertson-Smith undertook his investigations into the rites of the ancient Semites (and was dismissed from Oxford as a heretic for his pains) can be looked at as but a circuitous, even devious, approach to a rational analysis of our own situation, an evaluation of our own religious traditions while seeming to evaluate only those of exotic others.

The case is no different here. Moving from the special circumstances of Indonesia and Morocco to the new states in general, I hope to raise the suspicion that their predicament is also our own, that what they face we face, however differently we may formulate it or phrase our responses. I am not sure whether this will serve the Terry Foundation's stated purpose of "building the truths of science and philosophy into the structure of a broadened and purified religion," something I am not altogether certain is a good idea. But it ought at least to show those who would attempt such a valiant enterprise just what it is they are up against.

2. The Classical Styles

All the social sciences suffer from the notion that to have
named something is to have understood it, but nowhere is this
more true than in the comparative study of religion. There, the
overvaluation of classificatory modes of thought, the pigeonhole
disease, has grown to such alarming proportions that one sus-
pects some deeper passion to bring perverse phenomena to comforting terms is at work. Ask most people what they know of
comparative religion and, if they know anything at all, it will be
that there are such nebulous things abroad in the world as animism, animatism, ancestor worship, totemism, shamanism, mysticism, fetishism, saint worship, demonology, and even, a particular favorite of mine, dendrolatry, which, should your Greek be
rusty, means the adoration of trees and is said to be especially
prevalent in India.

In itself, naming things is of course a useful and necessary occupation, especially if the things named exist. But it is hardly much
more than a prelude to analytic thought. And when, as in the
case of comparative religion, it has not even been elaborated into
some form of systematics, an organized taxonomy (as, indeed,
given the ad hoc nature of the whole enterprise, it cannot be), it
suggests relationships among things categorized together which
have not in fact actually been discovered and asserted but only
sensed and insinuated. Aside from the simple question of whether
there really are any pigeons in all of these pigeonholes—any den-
drolators practicing dendrolatry in arcane dendrolatological ceremonies—the mere multiplication of generalized cover terms leads
to a tendency to assume that whatever is in a particular sort of
pigeonhole must be a particular sort of pigeon, else why should

he be in there? And so we get discussions of "animism" or "totem-ism" or (my particular concern here and my reason for bringing all this up) "mysticism," governed by a premise that has not been earned: that the first step toward a scientific comprehension of religious phenomena is to reduce their diversity by assimilating them to a limited number of general types. To my mind, and given my view of what such comprehension consists of, this is actually the first step toward denaturing our material, toward substituting cliché for description and assumption for analysis.

An attempt to characterize the classical religious styles in Morocco and Indonesia in such a way as to compare them effectively brings one face to face with precisely this issue. Both these styles were strongly marked by beliefs and practices one can only call—and indeed almost everyone has called—"mystical." But what "mystical" means in the two cases turns out to be very far from the same thing. To overcome this difficulty by generalizing the notion of mysticism so as to obscure these contrasts in the hope of finding broader, more abstract resemblances seems a most unpromising strategy, for to move away from the concrete details of the two cases is also to move away from the place where any general truth we might discover must necessarily lie. If, however, we use a concept like "mysticism"—or "mystic" or "mystical"—not to formulate an underlying uniformity behind superficially diverse phenomena, but to analyze the nature of that diversity as we find it, then pursuing the different meanings the concept takes in different contexts does not dissolve its value as an ordering idea but enriches it. As with other open-ended notions like "man" or "politics" or "art"—or, indeed, "religion"—the further we go into the details of the phenomena to which the notion can plausibly be applied, the more vivid, the more illuminating, and, its limits located, its differentiations determined, the more exact it becomes. In this area of study, at least, the interest of facts lies in their variety, and the power of ideas rests not on the degree to which they can dissolve that variety but the degree to which they can order it.

With this prelude, then, let me, as a way into our subject, relate two brief stories, legends actually, though they concern historical personages, one a sixteenth-century Javanese prince popularly regarded to have been instrumental in the Islamization of his country, and the other a seventeenth-century half-Berber, half-Arab religious scholar who has been transformed into an important Moroccan saint. These men are metaphors. Whatever they originally were or did as actual persons has long since been dissolved into an image of what Indonesians or Moroccans regard to be true spirituality. As such they are but two among dozens of similar figures, enveloped in similar legends, who might have been chosen. But had others been chosen, the contrast I wish to bring out would have been on the same order: between a spirituality, or "mysticism" if you wish, which consists in psychic balance and one which consists in moral intensity.

The Indonesian figure is Sunan Kalidjaga, the most important of the so-called "nine apostles," *wali sanga,* traditionally considered to have introduced Islam into Java and, more or less singlehandedly and without resort to force, converted its population to the new creed. As an historical personage, Sunan Kalidjaga, like the other apostles, is dim to the point where a few scholarly doubts have been raised as to whether he existed at all. But as an exemplary hero, the man who more than any other is regarded as having brought Java from the shadow-play world of *djaman Indu,* "Hindu times," to the scriptural one of *djaman Islam,* "Islamic times," he is to this day an extremely vivid figure in the popular mind—one of a long series of "culture renewers," some before, some after him, who through the sheer depth and purity, the unshakable stability of their inner lives, have carried the entire society forward into a new phase of spiritual existence.

Kalidjaga is said to have been born the son of a high royal official of Madjapahit, the greatest and, a few minor enclaves aside, the last of the Indonesian Hindu-Buddhist kingdoms. Madjapahit, whose capital lay on the lower reaches of the Brantas River of Eastern Java about fifty miles back from the coast, dominated the archipelago and the regions around it through most of the fourteenth and fifteenth centuries. During the first half of the sixteenth century, the princes of the burgeoning trade principalities along Java's northern coast—Bantem, Tjeribon, Demak, Djapara, Tuban, Grisik, Surabaya—went, one by one, over to Islam and, the spell of thearchic kingship broken, seceded, leaving Madjapahit a court without a country, an hieratic shell which soon collapsed entirely.

The breakaway harbor states struggled bitterly among themselves, but by the third decade of the sixteenth century one of them, Demak, managed to attain a certain ascendancy and become the center, the primus inter pares, of the whole newly forming Islamic coastal civilization. Its preeminence was short lived, however—less than thirty years—because it rested on the fact that, virtually alone among the harbor states, Demak had been able to develop its agricultural hinterland, and, once developed, this hinterland immediately rebelled in turn. Mataram, originally an inland province of Demak located near where Jogjakarta is today, that is to say, in the very heart of agrarian Java, first declared its independence and then, gathering political force and religious purpose, swallowed not only Demak itself but most of the other north coast kingdoms as well. Java's political center of gravity was thus moved back, after its short-lived displacement to the coast, to its traditional, and one is tempted to say natural, locus in the rice land interior, and Mataram became, until the Dutch reduced it in the eighteenth century, the greatest of the Islamized states of Indonesia, a Muslim Madjapahit.

It was in this "time without order," as the Javanese call it, "the time between times," when the Indic civilization was dissolving and the Islamic forming, that Kalidjaga lived. He left the failing Madjapahit capital as a young man, moving to one of the liveliest of the arriviste harbor states, Djapara, where he met and became a student of (that is, was converted to Islam by) another of the apostles, Sunan Bonang. From there he moved further along the coast, wandering from town to town, until he arrived at Tjeribon, where he married the daughter of yet a third apostle, Sunan Giri; and finally he gravitated to Demak where he is conceived to have played a central political role in the rise, breakaway, and expansion of Mataram. He is said to have been teacher and guide both to the original leader of the Mataram revolt against Demak, Senapati, and to the independent state's greatest king, Sultan Agung, and to have spread the new faith among the masses of the Javanese heartland. His career was thus his country's history: abandoning the dying, discredited, desanctified Madjapahit, he passed through the politico-religious upheavals of the transitional harbor states to arrive at the renascent spirituality of Mataram, a human recapitulation of a social transformation.

In short, as a symbol, a materialized idea, Sunan Kalidjaga connects Indic Java with Muslim Java, and therein lies his interest both for us and for the Javanese. Whatever the facts may be, he is seen as the bridge between two high civilizations, two historical epochs, and two great religions: that of the Madjapahit Hindu-Buddhism in which he grew up and that of the Mataram Islam which he fostered. For the Javanese he is (or, more exactly, his life is) the meaningful link between a world of god-kings, ritual priests, and declamatory shrines and one of pious sultans, Koranic scholars, and austere mosques. It is therefore of some value to look a little more closely at the story, as the Javanese tell it, of that conversion in Djapara where, like Saul in Damascus, a mystical experience led him, midway in the journey of his life, to change his religion, his name, and, tuning the traditions of an established civilization to the aspirations of an emerging one, his wordly destiny.

The actual conversion was not, however, exactly Pauline in spirit. When Sunan Kalidjaga arrived in Djapara (I summarize now my informants' renderings of the tale, which do not agree in every detail but present a common pattern), he was a fairly accomplished ne'er-do-well named Raden Djaka Sahid—Lord Young Man Sahid. At home he had been an habitual thief, not averse to stealing from his own mother in order to drink, whore, and in particular, gamble. When his mother's money was gone, he abandoned her impoverished and set out to steal from the general public, becoming finally a highwayman of such renown that men were afraid to go to the market in Djapara for fear of being held up by him.

It was at this time that Sunan Bonang, said by some informants to be an Arab and in any case a Muslim, came to Djapara. He was dressed in gorgeous clothes, draped with expensive jewels, and his cane was of solid gold. As he walked the streets of Djapara thus set out, he naturally attracted the professional attentions of Raden Djaka Sahid, who stopped him and, brandishing a dagger, demanded his jewels, his clothes, and his golden cane. But Bonang was not afraid, and indeed he simply laughed. He said, "Lo, Sahid [whose name he knew though he had never seen or heard of him before], don't always be wanting this thing and that thing and the other thing; desire is pointless. Do not be attached to wordly goods; we live but for a moment. Look! There is a tree of money."

And when Sahid looked behind him he saw that the banyan tree had turned to gold and was hung with jewels, and he was astounded. In fact, he was instantly convinced—"he became aware," as the Javanese idiom, always phenomenological in such matters, puts it; "realized," we would say—that material goods, the things of this world, were as nothing compared to the power of Sunan Bonang. Then he thought to himself, "This man can turn trees into gold and jewels and yet he does not seek riches." And he said to Bonang that he no longer wished to rob, drink, wench, gamble, and so on; he wanted only the sort of spiritual knowledge that Bonang had, wanted very much to be instructed by him in his "science." Bonang said, "All right, but it is very difficult. Do you have the strength of will, the steadfastness, the endurance?" When Sahid said he would persist till death, Bonang merely replied, "Wait here by the side of the river until I come back." And he went on his way.

Sahid waited there by the side of the river for years—some say ten, some say twenty, others even thirty or forty—lost in thought.

Trees grew up around him, floods came and covered him with water and then receded, crowds passed him by, jostling him as they went, buildings were built and torn down, but he remained unmoved in his trance. At length Bonang returned and saw that Sahid (he had some difficulty locating him amid the trees) had indeed been steadfast. But instead of teaching him the doctrines of Islam he merely said, "You have been a good pupil, and as a result of your long meditation you now know more than I do," and he began to ask him questions, advanced questions, on religious matters, which the uninstructed pupil answered immediately and correctly. Bonang then gave him his new name, Kalidjaga—"he who guards the river"—and told him to go forth and spread the doctrine of Islam, which he then did with unsurpassed effectiveness. He had become a Muslim without ever having seen the Koran, entered a mosque, or heard a prayer—through an inner change of heart brought on by the same sort of yoga-like psychic discipline that was the core religious act of the Indic tradition from which he came. His conversion was not a matter of a spiritual or moral change following upon a decisive change in belief (which is how *Webster's* defines the word), but a willed spiritual and moral change which eventuated in an almost accessorial change in belief. Sunan Kalidjaga became a Muslim because he had reformed; he did not reform because he had become a Muslim. His redemption, if that is what it should be called, was a self-produced inner state, a willed mood. And his Islam, if that is what *it* should be called, was but a public faith he was assigned, as he was assigned his professional name and his cultural mission.

The Moroccan figure I want to strike off against Kalidjaga is Abū 'Alī Al-Ḥasan ben Mas'ūd Al-Yusi, popularly known as Sīdī Laḥsen Lyusi. Lyusi, who is much more of a fully historical figure than Kalidjaga (a fact which has not, however, inhibited his mythologization), was born in an obscure tribe of transhumant shepherds—their very name means "the solitary ones"—in the Middle Atlas Mountains in 1631. He was apparently a Berber, but popular legend (which Lyusi himself launched by claiming his surname was a corruption of the Arabic Yussef) has it that his father was not only an Arab but indeed a descendant, by way of Idris II, the founder of Fez, of the Prophet Muhammed—what Muslims called a *sheríf*. He died (factually in Fez, by legend self-exiled in the forests of the Middle Atlas) in 1691, so that if Kalidjaga's career coincided with the rise of Mataram out of the formless struggles of the harbor states, Lyusi's coincided with the rise of the Alawite dynasty—the one which still reigns in Rabat—out of the sectarian anarchy of the Maraboutic Crisis. Both men lived in times when their societies were moving, hesitantly, painfully, and, in the nature of the case, quite incompletely, toward form, after having been disrupted by fundamental religio-political upheaval. But where Kalidjaga attempted to direct that movement by representing it in his consciousness, creating in microcosm the harmony sought for in macrocosm, Lyusi attempted to direct it by struggling against it, by exposing in his teachings and his actions the internal contraditions it was seeking desperately to contain. The first approach is essentially aesthetic; it portrays its ideal. The second is essentially moral; it commands it.

The Maraboutic Crisis which had broken out in the fifteenth century with the collapse of the last of the great Berber dynasties, the Merinids, came during Lyusi's lifetime, the seventeeth century, more or less to an end. This is not to say that maraboutism did, for saint worship is an historical constant in Morocco, existing as a powerful popular force under the Berber dynasties as it exists today. What was different during these two hectic centuries from those that preceded and followed them was not that Moroccans worshipped saints, but that such worship attained a luxuriance of political expression it had not been able to achieve before and was unable to regain after. Morocco splintered, in this period, into a collection of larger and smaller polities centered around holy men of one sort or another (leaders of Sufi sects, local Koranic teachers, self-appointed evangelists, wandering ascetics, and the like)—a proliferation of zealous, insular, intensely competitive hagiocracies, sometimes called maraboutic states, though most of them were more like utopian communities, aggressive utopian communities, than proper states. By the beginning of the seventeenth century, Morocco had become a spiritual cauldron in which, to quote Jacques Berque, "doctrinal ardor and rustic violence produced vivid personalities, some benefic, some not, locked in a combat cruel and picturesque."

It was into this caldron that, somewhere around his twentieth year, Lyusi descended from the relative isolation of his mountain homeland to become, in legend anyway, first a pilgrim, then a rebel, and finally a saint. For the whole of his adult life he wandered, again rather like Kalidjaga, from one center of political and spiritual turmoil to another, from the powerful but fading maraboutic states of Dila or Tazerwalt to the stagnant scholastic centers of Fez and Marrakech, from Sufi sheikh to Sufi sheikh, from tribe to tribe, town to town, region to region. He never seems to stop moving, never comes to rest, never—*unlike* Kalidjaga—finds his center, stabilizes his self. "My heart is scattered through my country," he writes in a piercing poem Berque has recovered for us,

> One part is in Marrakech, in doubt;
> Another in Halfun; another in Meknes with my books;
> Another in the Fazaz; another in Mulwiya [his home-
>   land] among my tribesmen;
> Another in the Gharb, among my friends of the town
>   and of the countryside
> O God, reunite them. No one can do it but You.
> O God, put them back in place

Where Kalidjaga sought (and found) peace in immobility, in an iron calm, at, to use Eliot's figure, the still point of the turning world, Lyusi, despite the petitions to God to put him back together, seems hardly to have sought it at all, in this world anyway. Like his countrymen (for this contrast, too, is general, a characteristic not merely of our example figures but also of the peoples they are examples for) his natural mode of being was restlessness, his discipline mobility, and he sought to capture truth not by waiting patiently for it to manifest itself to his emptied consciousness, but by tirelessly and systematically tracking it down. He did not travel to find a new sanctuary because an old one had been breached; he traveled because, like his shepherd parents, he was a traveler.

In this lifelong pilgrimage of Lyusi's, two incidents stand out, at least in the popular mind, as defining the nature of his saintliness and thus of saintliness in general. The first is his discipleship to the famous pre-Saharan Sufi sheikh Aḥmed ben Nāṣir al-Dar'ī, founder of a very large order, the Nasiri, which, though somewhat subdued, is still quite important in Morocco. The second is his confrontation—collision is perhaps the more exact word —with the great consolidator of the Alawite dynasty, Morocco's Akbar Sultan Mulāy Ismā'il ben 'Ali. As with Kalidjaga, I will rely mainly on my informants' renderings, for what they lack in historical accuracy they more than make up for in cultural penetration.

When, the story goes, Lyusi arrived at Tamgrut, the desert-edge oasis where ben Nasir was teaching, he found the old man critically ill with a loathsome disease, perhaps, from the sound of it, smallpox. The sheikh called his students to him, one by one, and asked them to wash his nightshirt. But each was so repelled by the sickness, so disgusted by his and the nightshirt's appearance, as well as afraid for his own health, that he refused to do it, or indeed to come any more into the sheikh's presence.

Lyusi had just arrived and was unknown to the sheikh, and everyone else, and so was not called. But he approached ben Nasir unbidden and said, "My teacher, I will wash your clothes." Given the shirt, he took it to a spring where he rinsed it and, wringing it out, drank the foul water thus produced. He returned to the sheikh, his eyes aflame, not with illness, for he did not fall sick, but as though he had drunk a powerful wine. Thus all knew that Lyusi was not, or anyway not any longer, an ordinary man, that he had what the Moroccans call *baraka*—one of those resonant words it is better to talk about than to define, but which for the moment we can call, inadequately, "supernatural power," and the possession of which makes a saint, a marabout. The elements of this spiritual transformation (for although there was no formal change of religious allegiance involved, it was as much of a new birth as Kalidjaga's by the riverside) are worth noting: extraordinary physical courage, absolute personal loyalty, ecstatic moral intensity, and the almost physical transmission of sanctity from one man to another. That, rather than stoical quietism, is what spirituality has, for the most part, meant in Morocco.

The confrontation with Sultan Mulay Ismail came only some thirty years later, after a lifetime's wandering from maraboutic center to maraboutic center. (He was in the most powerful of these, Dila, when the Alawites, under Ismail's brother, finally sacked it in 1668 and put an end to two centuries of molecular politics.) It took place in the Sultan's monumental new capital at Meknes, a kind of Moorish Kremlin, designed to convince both him and his subjects that Morocco had a proper dynasty again. And, at least as it is related, it forms a folktale commentary on the delicate relationship between strong-man politics and holy-man piety, the continuously sought but only sporadically effected effort to fuse the force of the warrior and the virtue of the saint, which, as I have said, is the leitmotiv of Moroccan history.

When Lyusi, by then one of the country's most illustrious scholars, arrived in Meknes, Mulay Ismail received him as an honored guest, fed him and housed him, and brought him into his court as his spirutual advisor. The Sultan was at that time building a large wall around the city, and the people working on it, slaves and others, were being treated cruelly. One day a man fell ill while working and was sealed into the wall where he fell. Some of the workers came secretly to Lyusi to tell him of this and to complain of their treatment generally. Lyusi said nothing to Mulay Ismail, but when his supper was brought to his chambers he proceeded to break all the dishes, one by one, and he continued to do this, night after night, until all the dishes in the palace had been destroyed.

When the Sultan then asked what had happened to all his dishes, the palace slaves said, "That man who is our guest breaks them when we bring his food."

The Sultan ordered Lyusi to be brought to him:

> "*Salām 'Alaikum.*"
> " *'Alaikum Salām.*"
> "My Lord, we have been treating you like the guest of God, and you have been breaking all our dishes."
> "Well, which is better—the pottery of Allah or the pottery of clay?" [i.e. I break plates, human creations, but you break people, God's creations.]

and he proceeded to upbraid Mulay Ismail for his treatment of the workers who were building his wall.

The Sultan was unimpressed and said to Lyusi, "All I know is that I took you in, gave you hospitality [a deeply meaningful act in Morocco], and you have caused all this trouble. You must leave my city." Lyusi left the palace and pitched his tent in the graveyard just outside the city near where the wall was being built. When the Sultan heard of this he sent a messenger to the saint to ask why, since he had been told to leave his, the Sultan's, city, he had not in fact done so. "Tell him," Lyusi said, "I have left your city and I have entered God's."

Hearing this, the Sultan was enraged and came riding out himself on his horse to the graveyard, where he found the saint praying. Interrupting him, a sacrilege in itself, he called out to him, "Why have you not left my city as I ordered?" And Lyusi replied, "I went out of your city and am in the city of God, the Great and the Holy." Now wild with fury, the Sultan advanced to attack the saint and kill him. But Lyusi took his lance and drew a line on the ground, and when the Sultan rode across it the legs of his horse began to sink slowly into the earth. Frightened, Mulay Ismail began to plead to God, and he said to Lyusi, "God has reformed me! God has reformed me! I am sorry! Give me pardon!" The saint then said, "I don't ask for wealth or office, I only ask that you give me a royal decree acknowledging the fact that I am a sherif, that I am a descendant of the Prophet and entitled to the appropriate honors, privileges, and respect." The Sultan did this and Lyusi left, still in fear for his safety, fleeing to the Middle Atlas forests, where he preached to the Berbers (and against the king) and ultimately died, was buried, and transformed into a *siyyid*, a man around whose tomb an elaborate devotional cult has developed.

Two men, two cultures; and like those cultures, at one and the same time sharply different yet curiously similar. Their differences are apparent, as differences usually are. One a townsman; the other a rustic. One a displaced aristocrat attempting to sustain his status; the other an ordinary tribesman attempting to raise himself above his origins. One a yogi and spiritually something of a chameleon, tuning surface features to novel settings while remaining inwardly inviolate; the other a puritan and something of a zealot, asserting the moral sovereignty of personal holiness in whatever setting at whatever cost. The similarities are more elusive, as similarities, at least when they are genuine and more than skin deep, usually are. They rest on two facts. First, both figures are profoundly conservative, defending received forms of religious consciousness in the face of radical social and political challenges to their continuation. And second, it is the increasing penetration of the very religious tradition to which they are ostensibly committed, Islam, that makes this defense both necessary and, as times passes, increasingly desperate. But these rather cryptic comments, summing up in a phrase religious development in Indonesia and Morocco to the end of the nineteenth century, demand a good deal of explication.

On the Indonesian side, the cultural tradition out of which Kalidjaga came and whose religious outlook he struggled to maintain after the tradition itself had disappeared was that of the great court centers of Indic Java. In attempting to summarize that outlook in a few words, I would like to reduce it to a series of doctrines, though in fact there were no such doctrines in the sense of explicit formulations dogmatically asserted, but only in the sense of implicit principles in terms of which religious life was conducted. The first and most important of these I will call "The Doctrine of the Exemplary Center"; the second, "The Doctrine of Graded Spirituality"; and the third, "The Doctrine of the Theater State." Together they make up a world view and an ethos which is elitist, esoteric, and aesthetic, and which remains, even after the adaptations and reformulations forced upon it by four hundred years of Islamization, three hundred of colonial domination, and twenty of independence, a powerful theme in the contemporary Indonesian consciousness.

By "The Doctrine of the Exemplary Center," I mean the notion that the king's court and capital, and at their axis the king himself, form at once an image of divine order and a paradigm for social order. The court, its activities, its style, its organization, its whole form of life, reproduces, albeit imperfectly, the world of the gods, provides a visible likeness of an invisible realm. And because it does this, it also provides an ideal toward which life outside the court, in the kingdom as a whole, ought properly to aspire, upon which it should seek to model itself, as a child models itself upon a father, a peasant upon a lord, a lord upon a king, and a king upon a god.

Indeed, from a religious point of view, that is the court's basic function and justification—to disseminate civilization by displaying it, to shape society by presenting it with a microcosmic expression of macrocosmic form which it can attempt, as well as it is able, to imitate. The welfare of the country proceeds from the excellence of its capital, the excellence of the capital from the brilliance of its court, the brilliance of its court from the spirituality of its king. When Prapanca, the great court poet of Madjapahit, the author of the *Negarakertagama*, seeks to express its glory and that of its ruler, he depicts the entire realm as a copy of its capital—the thousands of peasant houses are likened to the manors of the courtiers disposed around the royal compound; the outer provinces, grown happy and quiet, to the cultivated land along the city's edge; the unpopulated forests and mountains, now safe for travel and relaxation, to its tranquil parks. The capital is like the sun, he says elsewhere in the poem; the country like its halo.

The notion that spirituality is not equally distributed among men but nicely apportioned according to position along the gradient of socio-political rank which runs from king to peasant follows from this glowing center view of authority almost as a logical corollary. The capacity for the kind of inward focusing of consciousness upon the sources of one's existence—that is, upon the ultimate—that Kalidjaga demonstrated not only varies from one person to another but does so in terms of a very finely calibrated status hierarchy; it is no accident that he was born a lord. The mere fact of human inequality has, in and of itself, metaphysical significance: the difference between "high" and "low" is at the same time the difference between those more able to detach themselves from the temporal so as to contemplate the eternal and those less able, that is to say, between the relatively sacred and the relatively profane. Prestige and sanctity are interchangeable terms which, like highness and lowness, come in degrees, and the social ladder reaches toward the same culmination as religious meditation: nonbeing. "The retainer should honor the master," another Madjapahit text, a collection of rules concerning worship, declares, "the master should honor the headman, the headman should honor the lord, the lord should honor the prince, the prince should honor the priest, the priest should honor the godking, the god-king should honor the supernatural beings, the supernatural beings should honor the Supreme Nothingness."

There are a number of implications of such a view of things, not the least important of which is that the king, by the mere fact of being king, is the paramount sacred object. It is upon him that the whole system pivots, for he stands at the juncture of the divine and the human with, so to speak, a foot in each camp. Commonly this was expressed by indeed regarding him as the incarnation of a god, or, in the Buddhist variant, as a bodhisattva (or, often enough, as both). But the critical point is that in the ranking of men in terms of their capacity for spiritual enlightenment through disciplined self-inspection, their ease of access to ultimacy, he represents at once the apex, if one looks at the system from the bottom up, or the fountainhead, if, as is more in keeping with the exemplary center conception, one looks at it from the top down. Here, the problem was not fusing strong man and holy man— power and charisma were inherently correlated from the top of the society to the bottom. The problem was to extend the power by dramatizing the charisma, to magnify the sun so that it should cast a wider and more blinding halo.

The "Theater State" then, to complete the circle, is simply the concrete realization of this conception. The ritual life of the court —the mass ceremonies, the high-wrought art, the elaborate politesse—formed not just the trappings of rule but the substance of it. Spectacle was what the state was for; its central task was less to govern—a job the villagers largely accomplished for and among themselves—than to display in liturgical form the dominant themes of Javanese culture. The capital was a stage upon which the priests and nobles, headed by the king, presented an endless sacred pageant with respect to which the ordinary man was at once spectator, spear carrier and, through the tribute and service he was obliged to render, sponsor. The scale of ceremonial activity that any particular state could mount was the measure both of its hegemony—for the more effective the state's techniques for mobilizing men and materiel, the greater that scale could be —and of the degree to which it was indeed an exemplary center capable of evoking the attitude Prapanca claims "the whole of the Javanese country" had toward the "peerless" king of Madjapahit: "helpless, bowed, stooping, humble."

So long as the agrarian civilization of the great interior rice plains with its leisured courts competing for peasant surpluses continued, this elegant combination of quietism, ceremonialism, and hierarchism could continue also, for it both formulated the conditions of life as everyone from king to slave, if from different standpoints, doubtless with different sentiments, and perhaps even with different convincement, knew them, and provided a general interpretation, justification if you wish, of why they were that way. What it expressed in symbolic form men confronted in actual experience, and what men confronted in actual experience it lent a broader form and a deeper meaning to. This is circular. but religion, considered as a human phenomenon, is always like that. It draws its persuasiveness out of a reality it itself defines. The source of any creed's vitality, even one so implicit and un-codified as the Indo-Javanese, lies in the fact that it pictures the ultimate structure of existence in such a way that the events of everyday life seem repeatedly to confirm it. It is when this magi-cal circle is broken and religious concepts lose their air of simple realism, when the world as experienced and the world as imag-ined no longer seem to be mere elucidations of one another, that perplexities ensue.

It was precisely this sort of breaking of the circle that the rise of the north coast kingdoms must have caused, not only for nota-bles like Kalidjaga, but for large numbers of ordinary Javanese. It was not merely the intrusion of Islam—for that could have been, and in the upper classes was, easily absorbed without any fundamental change of view—but the sudden expansion of the trading classes, a tangled crowd of foreigners and locals, that pro-duced an element unassimilable to the Indic world view. There had been traders along the coasts, not merely of Java but of Su-matra, Borneo, and the Celebes as well, for centuries. But what was different about the development in the fifteenth and sixteenth centuries was that the center of political and economic power in the archipelago threatened to shift, for more than a century did shift, to such men. In the harbor states quantitative change induced qualitative. The trading groups, organized into separate ethnic quarters centered not upon the local court but on mosque and market, moved easily from one town to the next and in and out of the archipelago, and, too busy with commerce to be much concerned with either rank or ceremony, upset the status hier-archy, disrupted the theater state, and ignored the exemplary cen-ter—that is to say, instituted a social revolution.

With the appearance of Mataram, consciously modeling itself, despite its supposed Islamism, upon Madjapahit, the revolution was—temporarily, as it turned out—arrested. But by then it had proceeded far enough to introduce a new element into the Javanese and, as many of the traders were Outer Islanders, Indonesian social structure. Though for what at first must have been an overwhelming majority of the population the Indic world view continued under a nominal conversion to Islam, it was no longer without a rival—a rival that, as both commercial life and contact with centers of the Muslim world increased, grew steadily more powerful. A new theme—the tension between the spell of Madjapahit and the pull of the Koran—was introduced into Indonesian spiritual life, and what was to become a thoroughgoing differentiation of the country's religious tradition was begun.

The bulk of this differentiation, and thus the definitive formation of the classical religious style in Indonesia, took place in the three centuries, roughly 1530 to 1830, in which the country passed from being a spice shop for Europe to being a province of it. The establishment of Dutch hegemony, fought bitterly by Mataram but ultimately accomplished, cut the ground out from under the theater state tradition until it became mostly theater and very little state. The exemplary view of authority, the Nirvanic view of worship, and the blank-screen view of the divine, dressed now in Muslim guise, continued, and indeed in a curious way flourished. But those who held it were progressively transformed, not without incident, from intransigent oligarchs struggling to rebuild Madjapahit to pliant functionaries content to remember it.

The crushing of Mataram, essentially completed by the middle of the eighteenth century, led to a three-sided division of political labor in Indonesia, the distinctiveness, indeed the outright peculiarity, of which has not been sufficiently appreciated. Ultimate power, in the sense of sovereign force, was, of course, in Dutch hands, though the intensity with which it was asserted was not uniform over the archipelago. Day to day local administration, however, was almost everywhere in the hands of an indigenous civil service whose members were the heirs of the former ruling class, a kind of white-collar aristocracy. And the symbols of authority, the religio-cultural trappings of command, remained in the conquered courts and the disarmed nobility that manned them. A political system in which the sources of power, the instruments of rule, and the bases of legitimacy are so separately located would seem to be inherently unstable. But this one lasted, and in fact prospered, for about two hundred years. In part, this was because Dutch power was so overwhelming. But in part, too, it was because, however misted and remote, the Madjapahit sun still shone.

In fact, the reduction of the old courts to spiritual retreats for pensioned princes led to something of a cultural revival. Relieved, or largely so, of political concerns, the nobility could devote itself to perfecting the expressive side of authority—developing politesse to an almost obsessive complexity, refining the arts and indeed inventing new ones, and on the religio-philosophical side, cultivating the sort of languid mystagogy that tends to go with the sense that one is conserving, perhaps for not much longer, the relics of a vanished greatness. This Byzantine florescence, as G. P. Rouffaer aptly called it, formed in turn the source from which the aristocrats turned civil servants, now the vehicles if hardly the springs of authority in Indonesia, drew their life style, their social values, and their religious ideals. By the beginning of the nineteenth century the pattern of a bureaucratic gentry wielding power that it did not really have in the name of a cultural ideal that was not really regnant was characteristic not only of Java, but in somewhat modified and less intensive form, in the Outer Islands as well. Kalidjaga's palace-born heritage had passed to a class of office clerks.

But if government continued in Indonesia, so did trade; if Indicism, so Islam. The Dutch preemption of international, long-distance commerce—also the result of a protracted struggle, here more with agile merchants than stubborn kings—turned the indigenous traders inward to forge a domestic marketing system. And as this system was constructed, linking ultimately the whole archipelago in a continuous network of local trade, it carried with it the general tone of Koranic moralism (one hesitates to call it anything more substantial than that) that had accompanied the commercial explosion of the fourteenth and fifteenth centuries. If Indicism found its refuge in the bureau, Islam found its in the bazaar.

It was around this market network that the social institutions of Islam grew up in Indonesia, around it and out of it that an Islamic community in the proper sense of the term, an *umma*, crystallized. I will take up this story and this argument again and in more detail in the next chapter, when I turn to the problem of religious change in recent times. For now, the point I need to make is that orthodox Islamic consciousness—that is to say, a consciousness that at least desired to be and, however inexpertly or at third remove, actually attempted to be, Koranic—arose as a counter-tradition in Indonesia, a dissident point of view. The major religious style at the center of the society was (and somewhat reworked, still is) the theater state, exemplary center sort of outlook that generations of salaried Kalidjagas preserved by clothing it, thinly, in Arabian robes. Sunni Islam did not, today still does not, represent the spiritual mainstream in Indonesia. Its main strongholds on the fringes of the archipelago, un-Indicized enclaves in strategic pockets of Sumatra and the Celebes, and its main support in a marginal social class, itinerant market peddlers, it represented a challenge to that mainstream—a challenge which grew stronger and more insistent as it took deeper root and firmer outline and as a truly national society slowly formed, but a challenge whose force was scattered, whose appeal was circumscribed, and whose triumphs were local.

By the beginning of the nineteenth century, then, the major outlines of the Indonesian religious picture—a collage rather more than a picture—were set: at the heart, geographically as well as socially, the civil service version of (to coin a small neologism) Madjapahit exemplarism; along the margins and in the interstices, Indonesianized renditions of medieval Islam, now occult and emotional, now crabbed and scholastic, now dogmatic and puritan; and under, or behind, or around them both, the syncretistic folk religion of the mass of the peasantry—another matter about which I shall have more to say later on—which at once drew upon them, naturalized them, and resisted their intrusion. Never really reconciled to one another, these various strands were anyway reasonably well contained in a system which was less a synthesis than a sort of spiritual balance of power, a balance of power which rested on the kind of to-each-his-own arrangements which are possible in a society which is still more an assemblage of peoples and a collection of status groups loosely interrelated by a few pervasive institutions—magistracies and markets—than an integrated national community. When that sort of society was lost, so too was the balance.

Turning back, in this seesaw, now-Asia-now-Africa exposition, to Morocco, the established religious tradition which Lyusi was attempting to sustain in the face of social transformations was again that most succinctly summed up in the term "maraboutism." "Marabout" is a French rendering of the Arabic *murābiṭ*, which in turn derives from a root meaning to tie, bind, fasten, attach, hitch, moor. A "murābit" is thus a man tied, bound, fastened to God, like a camel to a post, a ship to a pier, a prisoner to a wall; or, more appropriately, as *ribāṭ*, another derivative, means a fortified sanctuary, a place of marabouts, like a monk to a monastery. In its various formations the word runs through the warp of Moroccan history. The first and greatest of the Berber empires, the founder of Marrakech and the conqueror of Andalusia, which we know in English as the Almoravids, was in fact Al Murābāṭin, "The Marabouts." Rabat, the capital of the country, derives from the "sanctuary" form, "ribat," which, in fact, it originally was. And so on: men, in some almost tangible sense, attached, bound, tied—perhaps the best word is shackled—to God (or anyway regarded to be so) were the immediate foci of religious emotion in "the Morocco that was." And even in the Morocco that is, their sentimental authority has far from disappeared.

The content of this bond, as well as the sign of its existence and the result of its operation, was, to return to a term I mentioned earlier, "baraka." Literally, "baraka" means blessing, in the sense of divine favor. But spreading out from that nuclear meaning, specifying and delimiting it, it encloses a whole range of linked ideas: material prosperity, physical well-being, bodily satisfaction, completion, luck, plenitude, and, the aspect most stressed by Western writers anxious to force it into a pigeonhole with mana, magical power. In broadest terms, "baraka" is not, as it has so often been represented, a paraphysical force, a kind of spiritual electricity—a view which, though not entirely without basis, simplifies it beyond recognition. Like the notion of the exemplary center, it is a conception of the mode in which the divine reaches into the world. Implicit, uncriticized, and far from systematic, it too is a "doctrine."

More exactly, it is a mode of construing—emotionally, morally, intellectually—human experience, a cultural gloss on life. And though this is a vast and intricate problem, what this construction, this gloss, comes down to, so at least it seems to me, is the proposition (again, of course, wholly tacit) that the sacred appears most directly in the world as an endowment—a talent and a capacity, a special ability—of particular individuals. Rather than electricity, the best (but still not very good) analogue for "baraka" is personal presence, force of character, moral vividness. Marabouts have baraka in the way that men have strength, courage, dignity, skill, beauty, or intelligence. Like these, though it is not the same as these, nor even all of them put together, it is a gift which some men have in greater degree than others, and which a few, marabouts, have in superlative degree. The problem is to decide who (not only, as we shall see, among the living, but also among the dead) has it, how much, and how to benefit from it.

The problem of who has it was indeed in some ways the central theological problem (if that is not too elegant a word for an issue which rarely rose above the oral and the practical) in classical Morocco. And to it two major classes of answers were, sometimes separately, sometimes simultaneously, given: what we may call the miraculous and the genealogical. Marabouthood, the possession of baraka, was indexed either by wonder-working, a reputation for causing unusual things to occur, or by supposed lineal descent from the Prophet. Or, as I say, by both. But though the two principles were often, after the seventeenth century perhaps most often, invoked together, they were yet separate principles, and in the tension between them can be seen reflected much of the dynamic of Moroccan cultural history. It is this tension, still powerful, that lies behind what might have seemed, when I recounted it, a curious twist to the end of the story of Lyusi and the Sultan —when, having convincingly impressed his miraculous powers upon the Sultan, this Berber mountaineer asks the Sultan to declare him a true descendant of the Prophet: a sherif. But, like Bonang's equally surprising refusal to teach Kalidjaga the Koran after his extravagant meditation, this incident is not a mere twist, an anticlimax. It is an image of a faith reacting to an unsettling shift of the ground on which, psychologically and sociologically, it has been questionlessly standing.

From a religious point of view, the rise of the Alawite dynasty, and especially its consolidation in the hands of Mulay Ismail, represented the assertion of the supremacy of the genealogical view of the basis of baraka over the miraculous; of the proposition that though sainthood is, naturally enough, accompanied by wonders, it is, conveniently enough, conveyed by blood. A sherifian dynasty, tracing its pedigree back patrilineally to Ali, the Prophet's son-in-law, it was dedicated, is dedicated, to the elevation of what Max Weber called hereditary charisma over what he called personal charisma and to the containment of baraka within the confines of a fixed and ordered status system. The Alawite answer to maraboutism was to license it; or anyway, to try to.

The sherifian principle of legitimacy was, of course, not new to Morocco in the seventeenth century. As I have mentioned several times before, the first proper king in Morocco, Idris II, claimed sherifian descent—his father, Idris I, having been driven from Baghdad by Harun Al Rachid. But Idris II's control was brief, about twenty years, and limited, confined to Fez and its environs. The Idrissids introduced the genealogical conception of baraka, but they could not establish it; visionary maraboutism soon swept it almost wholly away. The rise of first the Almoravid and then the Almohad kingdoms—the Almoravid in the eleventh and twelfth centuries, the Almohad in the twelfth and thirteenth —represents the emergence of personal charisma as a sovereign force in Morocco. The great Berber dynasties, the one founded by a messianic Saharan ascetic, the other by a Grand Atlas one, were, as Alfred Bel has remarked, sects before they were empires. Reformist sects, for they arose, on the religious level anyway, as reactions to the heresies and heterodoxies—Kharajism, Shiism, and just plain paganism—of Moroccan society. Fired by a passion for codified law perhaps only unlettered nomads can have, the Almoravids emerged from their ribats to fasten a Malakite orthodoxy on the whole of lowland Morocco—and, of course, to some extent on Spain as well. Fired by a distaste for the immorality which persisted within this legalistic shell, the Almohads— the name means, roughly, "unitarians," "absolute monotheists"— emerged from theirs to fasten upon it a God-frightened puritanism which, like the legalism, it never afterward lost. The whole process was much more complex than this—a matter of warring tribes, changing relations between the Islamic and Christian worlds, the opening of Barbary to the centers of Muslim thought, the incursion of Bedouin Arabs, and so on. But that it was self-made warrior saints—*hommes fétiches,* as Bel again so aptly calls them—who forged the uncreated conscience of Morocco, indeed forged Morocco itself, is beyond much doubt.

The Maraboutic Crisis, the collection of sectarian communities within which Lyusi was shaped, was but the debris of this tradition. The collapse, after a two-century holding action, of the third of the formative dynasties, the Merinids, fragmented political authority and scattered, so to speak, the hommes fétiches irregularly across the landscape. Rather like the Indonesian bazaar-states, though their origins were different and their styles contrasting, the Moroccan ribat-states were built out of the ruins of a civilization whose spiritual force outlived its political capacities. Both were, in the end, mere interludes, momentary deviations which, when they ended, seemed to have left everything the same but had in fact been revolutions. In Indonesia, the fateful change was the appearance of an alternative source of revelation —the Koran; in Morocco, it was the resurgence of an alternative principle of sanctity—sherifian descent.

The triumph of the Alawites, prefaced, actually, by the brief emergence of another sherifian dynasty, the Saadian, which failed to stabilize, faced the religious populism of men like Lyusi— men for whom baraka gravitated naturally to those, regardless of station, righteous enough to deserve it—with the contrasting notion of an hereditary spiritual patriciate. But no more than the Indic tradition dissolved in the face of Islamization in Indonesia did the wonder-working view of sainthood dissolve in the face of the genealogical in Morocco. In fact, surprising as it may seem, the two principles—that charisma was an individual talent and that it was a family patrimony—actually fused. Here, the outcome of the clash between an established outlook and an incoming doctrine was not a deepening differentiation of religious style but an increasing unification of it. "After the sixteenth century," Lévi-Provencal has written, "[religious] teaching, whether given at Fez or in the countryside, stamped the same distinctive imprint on the literature of the country. The culture of the Moroccan scholar took form in this period, and in the following, and it has not varied since."

And as with the literature and the scholar, so, more gradually and less completely, with the society as a whole. The views of different sorts of men—shepherds, farmers, artisans, traders, intellectuals, officials—concerning the nature of ultimate reality and true morality did not separate into distinct streams whose divergence increased as they progressed, but grew, somewhat paradoxically, given the intense social antagonisms among these various groups, closer together, became local variants on a pervading theme. That the story of Kalidjaga's confrontation with the new should end with intransigence in the guise of accommodation—Indicism maintained beneath an Islamic veneer—and that of Lyusi's with a capitulation in the guise of rebellion—the sherifian principle of religious legitimacy accepted in the course of a moral collision with its quintessential representative—is again superbly diagnostic. At the same time that Indonesia was moving toward spiritual cleavage, Morocco was moving, no less haltingly but also no less definitively, toward spiritual consolidation.

The whole process, the social and cultural stabilization of Moroccan maraboutism, is usually referred to under the rubric of "Sufism"; but like its most common gloss in English, "mysticism," this term suggests a specificity of belief and practice which dissolves when one looks at the range of phenomena to which it is actually applied. Sufism has been less a definite standpoint in Islam, a distinct conception of religiousness like Methodism or Swedenborgianism, than a diffuse expression of that necessity I mentioned in the last chapter for a world religion to come to terms with a variety of mentalities, a multiplicity of local forms of faith, and yet maintain the essence of its own identity. Despite the otherworldly ideas and activities so often associated with it, Sufism, as an historical reality, consists of a series of different and even contradictory experiments, most of them occurring between the ninth and nineteenth centuries, in bringing orthodox Islam (itself no seamless unity) into effective relationship with the world, rendering it accessible to its adherents and its adherents accessible to it. In the Middle East, this seems mainly to have meant reconciling Arabian pantheism with Koranic legalism; in Indonesia, restating Indian illuminationism in Arabic phrases; in West Africa, defining sacrifice, possession, exorcism, and curing as Muslim rituals. In Morocco, it meant fusing the genealogical conception of sanctity with the miraculous—canonizing *les hommes fétiches*.

Though essentially the same process and conducing toward a similar view of the way in which the divine appears in the world, this fusion took place, given the variety of social structures and, more especially, ecological situations, in a variety of institutional contexts, of which perhaps three were the most important: a cult of saints centered around the tombs of dead marabouts and involving the definition of sacred lineages comprised of each interred marabout's patrilineal descendants; voluntary religious organizations, usually called "brotherhoods" in English, organized into lodges and led by spiritual adepts, hierophants; and finally, the sherifian government itself, the Sultanate and the cult around it. We may call these three institutional settings, which were neither so distinct, so discordant, nor so independent of one another as has sometimes been represented, the *siyyid* complex, after the name given both to dead saints and to the tombs in which they are thought to be buried; the *zāwiya* complex, after the word for a lodge of a brotherhood and by extension for brotherhoods generally; and the *maxzen* complex, after the traditional term for the central government.

The siyyid complex was, and is, essentially a tribal phenomenon, though there have always been important urban siyyids as well, another evidence of the fact that tribal mentality does not stop at city walls in Morocco. The elements of the complex, considered in a normalized form to which almost any particular instance will not fully conform, include first, the tomb and its associated paraphernalia; second, the saint supposedly buried in the tomb; third, the living patrilineal descendants of the saint; and fourth, the cult by means of which the baraka embodied in the tomb, the saint, and the descendants are made available for human purposes.

The tomb (or in some cases, the cenotaph) is a squat, white, usually domed, block-like stone building set under a tree, on a hilltop, or isolated, like an abandoned pillbox, in the middle of an open plain. There are literally thousands of these graceless little structures scattered throughout the country (you can scarcely travel twenty miles without encountering one) but only a minority are, or ever have been, centers of developed cults, siyyids in the full sense of the term. The rest are mere sacred spots, places suitable for a passing prayer or an ad hoc offering.

The saint, who gives his name to the shrine, so that it is known as "Sidi Lahsen Lyusi," "Sidi Ahmed ben Yussef," or whatever, is almost always a quasi-mythological figure, heavily encrusted with miracle legends of the sort I related about Lyusi. Further, he is, in the more important cases anyway, at once a sherif, a descendant of the Prophet, and what Moroccans call the *mul blad*, the "owner" (in a spiritual sense) of the land, the region around the tomb, or in urban settings, of a craft, an occupation, a harbor, or the city as a whole—a patron saint rather on southern European and Latin American lines.

The living descendants of the saint, i.e. descendants in the male line, called *wulad siyyid*, "children of the siyyid," are, like him, also sherifs and are regarded as the contemporary stewards of the saint's sacredness, his baraka, having inherited it from him as he inherited it from the Prophet. This baraka is, however, unequally distributed among them so that, although all, even the women and children, are at least touched by it, only a few—two or three men in most cases, in many only one—will, as demonstrated by their wonder-working capacities, actually be saturated with it, be true living marabouts. Generations may even go by in which no true marabouts in this sense appear.

Finally, the cult that all this belief and legend supports consists of mobilizing the baraka embodied in the saint, in his tomb, and in his descendants, most especially those who are marabouts, for purposes ranging from the most petty to the most high. We need not pursue here the exact nature of these cults or the social uses to which they are put. Enough perhaps to say that on the ritual side they include everything from animal sacrifice and mass prayer to elaborate exchanges of hospitality and fancy horseback riding displays—the famous fantasias—and on the practical side everything from curing and soothsaying to judicial mediation and (in the past) military organization. The important points are that the siyyid complex was, for many Moroccans, ranging from mountain-dwelling Berbers, through lowland Arab farmers, to urban artisans, merchants, and even clerks, the main institutional mechanism for the mediation of Islam, and that at the center of this institution for transforming divine energies into mundane ones stood men in whom sacred genealogy and personal holiness, inherited baraka and, so to speak, characterological baraka, had met to produce genuine sainthood. "[The saints]," Ernest Gellner has written of a contemporary High Atlas Berber community, "are the Prophet's flesh and blood. Koranic propriety emanates from their essence, as it were. Islam *is* what they do. They *are* Islam." And the same outlook has obtained in a very large part of Morocco's population, Arab-speaking as well as Berber, urban as well as rural, for the whole of the last four centuries.

On the surface at least, the zawiya complex resembles rather more our usual image of Sufi practice than does the siyyid. Literally a retreat for the pious to gather in and carry out various sorts of spiritual exercises (it derives from a root meaning "corner" or "nook"), the term is also applied to the voluntary religious organization, the brotherhood, of which the particular lodge is, in a general sort of way, an affiliate. Dozens of these brotherhoods, large and small, local and pan-Moroccan, tediously formulistic and wildly ecstatic, have been established over the course of the Alawite period, some of them near the very beginning of it, like the Nasiri, some rather further on into it, like the Derqawi, some as late as the middle of the last century, like the Kittani. By 1939, nearly a fifth of the adult male population of French Morocco seems to have belonged to one or another of the twenty-three leading brotherhoods, about a sixth to the seven largest ones— huge, sprawling, denominational unions—alone. One ought not to take such figures as more than indicators and to remember that they are from 1939, not 1739. But that the zawiya was as important in the religious life of Morocco after the sixteenth century as the ribat (out of which it in large part grew) had been before, is clear enough.

Again, we need not detail the actual ceremonial practices which took place, and in sharply diminished but apparently again increasing degree still take place, in the zawiyas, except to say that they ranged from simple bead-telling repetition of the names of God, through blood sacrifice, to the more famous sort of whirling dervish performances—dancing with swords, playing with fire, charming snakes, mutual flagellation, and so on. It was, in any case, the particular rite, the procedure or method, *ṭarīqa* in the Muslim idiom, which gave any particular brotherhood whatever overall unity it had, made a given lodge Derqawi rather than Qadiri, or Qadiri rather than Tijani. Beyond this, the translocal organization was commonly loose in the extreme, a formless fellowship of the vaguely like-minded. Socially, the zawiya was, virtually everywhere and in all orders, primarily a local affair, a true nook. Its commanding figure was not the distant head of the whole order, when indeed there was such, but, connecting (to adapt a phrase of Berque's) forces infinitely parochial to ends infinitely vast, the chapter sheikh.

For the members of the particular zawiya, the sheikh (or sheikhs, for on occasion there could be more than one) was both the legitimate teacher of the order's technique, having himself learned it from such a teacher, who had learned it from such a teacher, and so on back to the founder of the order himself, and the man among them who, by means of the thus mastered technique, had approached most closely to a state of genuine holiness. As not all descendants of saints were sherifs, so neither were all zawiya sheikhs, but as with wulad siyyid, the more important among them almost inevitably were taken to be such; or, conversely, men whose Prophetic descent was already established were markedly more likely to become sheikhs in the first place. Some brotherhoods were organized around the core of a large sherifian clan to begin with; others were founded and perpetuated by men, like Lyusi, whose families had not previously made claim to sherifian descent but who, now that they had broken into the country's religious elite, took a more spiritual view of their ancestry. In either case, he who had attained any great amount of baraka from his own spiritual efforts—chanting verses or licking hot pokers—tended almost always to claim to have it also, so to speak, genetically.

As for the Sultanate, I shall have a good deal more to say about it in the next chapter, when I turn to the vicissitudes of our classical religious styles in modern times, for it is there, more than in any other Moroccan institution, that the contradictions implicit in an Islam scriptural in theory but anthropolatrous in fact have come home to roost. Here it is necessary only to point out that traditionally the Moroccan king has been in fact himself an homme fêtiche, a man alive with charisma of both the hereditary and personal sort. His legitimacy, his moral right to rule, derived concurrently from the fact that he was an Alawite sherif and that he was regarded by the religious adepts around the throne as the member of the ruling family spiritually most fit to hold the office. Once chosen he became therefore not just a ruler, but the center of a royal cult: the official religious leader of the country, the supreme expression of the sacredness of Prophetic descent, and the possessor of large and undefined magical powers. That, as with Mulay Ismail, the strong-man aspects of his role inevitably clashed with and usually dominated the holy-man aspects is both true and, for an understanding of the nature of the Moroccan state, critical. But it is just this fact, that it is difficult to play the monarch and the saint at the same time, which made (and, I daresay, makes) the cult so necessary.

The elements of the royal cult included the patronage of religious scholars in the great imperial cities, much as Mulay Ismail patronized Lyusi until the latter began to break his plates; the celebration of certain ceremonies on the main Muslim feast days and certain other holidays connected with his reign; the appointment of Islamic judges and other religious officials; the public veneration of the founder of the Alawite dynasty at his tomb in southern Morocco; the pronouncement of the Friday sermon in the Sultan's name; and so on. Again, the details do not matter here. The point is that baraka clung to the Sultan, and to certain members of his staff, the Maxzen, as it clung to certain descendants of saints and certain chiefs of brotherhoods. Despite their enormous differences in status, power, and function, and despite the fact that they were all in more or less open opposition to one another, they were, from the religious point of view, all the same

sort of figures. Popular saint worship, sufist doctrine (both Spanish and Middle Eastern), and the sherifian principle all flowed
together, like a swelling stream, into a single precut spiritual
channel: maraboutism.

"Mysticism," "piety," "worship," "belief," "faith," "sacredness,"
"tradition," "virtue," "spirituality," even "religion" itself—all
these words we use, as we must, for there are no others by means
of which we can talk intelligibly about our subject—thus turn
out, when we compare the way in which each of our peoples
came, on the whole, to develop a characteristic conception of what
life was all about, a conception they called Islamic, to mean
rather different things in the two cases. On the Indonesian side,
inwardness, imperturbability, patience, poise, sensibility, aesthet-
icism, elitism, and an almost obsessive self-effacement, the radical dissolution of individuality; on the Moroccan side, activism,
fervor, impetuosity, nerve, toughness, moralism, populism, and
an almost obsessive self-assertion, the radical intensification of
individuality. What can one say when one confronts a Javanese
quietist like Kalidjaga with a Berber zealot like Lyusi, except that
though both may be Muslims and mystics, they are certainly
rather different sorts of Muslims and different sorts of mystics?
Is it not true, as someone has remarked, that the more we plunge
into particulars the less we know anything in particular? Is the
comparative study of religion condemned to mindless descriptiv-
ism and an equally mindless celebration of the unique?

I think not. The hope for general conclusions in this field lies
not in some transcending similarity in the content of religious
experience or in the form of religious behavior from one people
to another, or one person to another. It lies in the fact, or what I
take to be a fact, that the field over which that content and that
behavior range is not a mere collection of unrelated ideas and
emotions and acts, but an ordered universe, whose order we shall

discover precisely by comparing, with some circumstantiality, cases drawn from different parts of it. The central task is to discover, or invent, the appropriate terms of comparison, the appropriate frameworks within which to view material phenomenally disparate in such a way that its very disparateness leads us into a deeper understanding of it. It would be incautious of me, at this point, to promise too much, or indeed to promise anything. But it is, in any case, an attempt to develop, step by step, and empirically rather than deductively, such a framework, to which this book is dedicated. What, after all, Kalidjaga and Lyusi have in common is what planets and pendulums have in common: looked at in the proper light, their very differences connect them.

3. The Scripturalist Interlude

The notion that religions change seems in itself almost a heresy. For what is faith but a clinging to the eternal, worship but a celebration of the permanent? Has there ever been a religion, from the Australian to the Anglican, that took its concerns as transient, its truths as perishable, its demands as conditional? Yet of course religions do change, and anyone, religious or not, with any knowledge of history or sense for the ways of the world knows that they have and expects that they will. For the believer this paradox presents a range of problems not properly my concern as such. But for the student of religion it presents one, too: how comes it that an institution inherently dedicated to what is fixed in life has been such a splendid example of all that is changeful in it? Nothing, apparently, alters like the unalterable.

On the secular level, the resolution of this paradox lies in the fact that religion is not the divine, nor even some manifestation of it in the world, but a conception of it. Whatever the really real may be really like, men make do with images of it they take, if they are faithful, as both depictions of it and guides for relating themselves to it. And which images, if any, seem revelatory and directive in this way is a function of place, as I tried to show in the last chapter, and of time, as I shall try to show in this. What happens to a people generally happens also to their faith and to the symbols that form and sustain it. Between the men I used in the last chapter as figurations of Indonesian and Moroccan spirituality in classical times, Kalidjaga and Lyusi, and those I shall use (in a somewhat different way) in this, President Sukarno and Sultan Muhammed V, as expressions of it in ours, lie the industrial revolution, Western intrusion and domination, the decline of the aristocratic principle of government, and the triumph of radical nationalism. What is surprising is not that there are differences between the two sets of portraits but that there are any resemblances.

But of course what we are interested in is not the mere differences between the past and the present but the way in which the former grew into the latter, the social and cultural processes which connect them. It is, indeed, a long way from precolonial Demak or Meknes to postcolonial Djakarta or Rabat. The blindest traditionalist sees that. The problem is to understand how, given such beginnings, we have arrived, for the moment, at such endings.

For accomplishing this task, the scientific explanation of cultural change, our intellectual resources are rather meager. Systematic discussions of the transformation of societies from what we gather they used to be like to what they seem now to be like generally follow one or another of a small number of strategies, which we may call the indexical, the typological, the world-acculturative, and the evolutionary.

The simplest of these is the indexical. A number of usually rather arbitrary indices of social advance—literacy, miles of paved road, per capita income, complexity of occupational structure—are set up and the society in question measured against them. Change consists of movement from scores farther away from those characteristic of fully industrialized societies toward ones closer to them. Even when quantitative measures are not used, the style of thinking is the same: religious change consists of (say) a decline in the magical element in worship and a rise in the devotional; political in (say) greater hierarchization of authority.

The typological approach involves setting up ideal-type stages —"primitive," "archaic," "medieval," "modern," or whatever— and conceiving change as a quantum-like breakthrough from one of these stages to the next. The career of a culture is portrayed in a series of snapshots taken at certain strategic points along it and arranged into a sequence at once temporal and logical.

In the world-acculturative approach, modernization is conceived in terms of borrowing from the West, and change is consequently measured by the degree to which values, ideas, and institutions which were, supposedly, perfected in the West—inner-worldly asceticism, the rule of law, or the small family—have diffused to the society in question and taken root there.

And in the evolutionary approach, now coming somewhat back into favor after a long eclipse, certain world-historical trends—increasing social differentiation, increasing control over energy, increasing individualism, increasing civility—are postulated as intrinsic to human culture, and a society's movement is measured in terms of the degree to which these trends have managed, against the lethargy of history, to express themselves.

To my mind, none of these approaches seems very promising. The indexical approach has its uses if you already have some idea of the nature of the processes you are investigating and if the indices are actually reflective of those processes. But as a way of getting at such processes in the first place, it is virtually valueless. One merely piles up indices by means of which to rank societies vis-à-vis one another without getting any clearer picture of the historical reality they are supposedly indices of.

The typological approach not only has the shortcoming that there are almost as many stage theories as there are stage theorists but, more critically, that it stresses a series of all-too-easily hypostatized static pictures of what is, again, actually a process, as though one were to try to understand the dynamics of human growth in terms of a procession of discontinuous biological states called infancy, childhood, adolescence, adulthood, and old age.

The world-acculturation model simply assumes what is in fact to be proven (and, as a matter of fact, is probably false)—that the development of what, in this idiom, are sometimes called "backward" societies consists of their approximation to the present condition of Western society and that this approximation is taking place by means of the more or less rapid diffusion of Western culture to them. Not only is there some doubt that this convergence upon Western patterns is occurring, but this approach provides no way to conceptualize the contribution of the recipient culture to the process of change in an other than passive way. Indeed, the established culture (and particularly the established religion) is, in this perspective, usually seen largely as a barrier to be overcome if change, that is to say, acculturation, is to occur.

And as for the evolutionary theories, they rest, when they are not so general as to be vacuous altogether—"a progress from disorganized simplicity to organized complexity," and that sort of thing—on the debatable idea that observed world-historical trends may be converted without further ado into world-historical laws, that the way history has happened to happen is the way it has had to happen.

These various stretegies for studying change may, of course, be combined, and some of them, for example the evolutionary and the typological, commonly are. But taken either together or separately, they seem to me to share a common defect: they describe the results of change, not the mechanisms of it. It may well be true that, compared to the Indonesia or Morocco of 1767, the Indonesia or Morocco of 1967 is more literate, has passed from being an "archaic" society to being a "premodern" one (whatever that might mean), has been deeply influenced by Western values, techniques, and modes of thought, and displays a much greater degree of social differentiation. But to say this is to raise questions, not to answer them. What we want to know is, again, by what mechanisms and from what causes these extraordinary transformations have taken place. And for this we need to train our primary attention neither on indices, stages, traits, nor trends, but on processes, on the way in which things stop being what they are and become instead something else.

In a sense, to pose the problem as I have—how our countries got to where they are from where they were—is to do history backward. Knowing, we think, the outcome, we look for how, out of a certain sort of situation obtaining in the past, that outcome was produced. There is a degree of danger in such a procedure, for it is all too easy to reverse the reasoning and to assume that given the past situation the present was bound to arise. This is, in fact, the mistake, a kind of logical howler reinforced by scientific dreams of grandeur, that the social evolutionists, and indeed all varieties of historical determinists, make. But the reasoning does not reverse. From the shape of things in Kalidjaga's or Lyusi's time thousands of futures were accessible. The fact that only one was reached proves not that the present was implicit in the past but that in history events are possibilities before they happen and certainties after. It is legitimate to look at a later state of affairs and isolate the forces that, with the finality of the already occurred, produced it out of a prior state of affairs. But it is not legitimate to locate those forces in the prior state itself, nor indeed to locate them anywhere but in the events through which they actually operated. Life, as Kierkegaard said, is lived forward but understood backward. For the historical sociologist, whose concern is general explanation, as opposed to the descriptive historian, whose concern is faithful portrayal, doing history backward is the proper way to do it.

So far as our topic, religious change in Indonesia and Morocco, is concerned, the great difference in the present situation over the one I described earlier is that the classical religious styles in each case—illuminationism and maraboutism—are no longer more or less alone in the field but are besieged on all sides by dissenting persuasions. Attacked from the spiritual left by secularism and, much more importantly, from the spiritual right by what I am going to call, in a perhaps slightly eccentric use of the term, "scripturalism," these main-line traditions not only no longer have the hegemony they once had, they do not even have the definition. They remain, in some general, overall, vaguely pervasive way, the basic religious orientations in their respective countries, the characteristic forms of faith. Substantively, they have not changed. What has changed, if one may speak anthropomorphically for the moment, is their sense that their dominance is complete and their position is secure. This is gone and, barring extraordinary developments, gone permanently. They, or more accurately their adherents, feel themselves embattled, at once the heritors of a tested vision and embarrassingly out of date. Piety remains, but assurance does not.

To describe the religious history of, say, the past one hundred and fifty years in Indonesia and Morocco is therefore to describe a progressive increase in doubt. But doubt of a peculiar kind. With some exceptions, which may or may not represent the wave of the future (my own inclination is to think not), there has been rather little increase in skepticism in the proper sense, in atheism and agnosticism. Nearly everyone in either country still holds beliefs one can, by almost any reasonable definition, call religious, and most hold a very great many. What they doubt, unconsciously and intermittently, is their belief—its depth, its strength, its hold upon them—not its validity. I hope I am not being too subtle or paradoxical here. I do not mean to be. The point I am trying to make is an elusive one; yet in my opinion, it is also an overwhelmingly important one. On the spiritual level, the big change between the days of Mataram and Mulay Ismail and today is that the primary question has shifted from "What shall I believe?" to "How shall I believe it?" In neither country have men yet come in any vast numbers to doubt God. But they have come, if not precisely in vast numbers in quite significant ones, to doubt themselves.

I attempted to phrase this point in the first chapter in terms of a distinction between "religiousness" and "religious-mindedness," between being held by religious convictions and holding them. Religious-mindedness, celebrating belief rather than what belief asserts, is actually a response, perhaps the most logical response, to the sort of doubt I am talking about. Given a dislocation between the force of classical symbols, which has lessened, and their appeal, which has not, or not as much, the indicated procedure is to base their validity on something other than their intrinsic coerciveness: namely, to be paradoxical one last time, their hallowedness—their spiritual reputation rather than their spiritual power.

The bulk of our two populations still considers either an inward search for psychic equilibrium or a moral intensification of personal presence the most natural mode of spiritual expression. The problem is that these days naturalness seems increasingly difficult actually to attain. Everything is growing terribly deliberate, willed, studied, *voulu*. Victims, in this dimension, anyway, of an altered social situation, a steadily increasing number of Indonesians and Moroccans are discovering that though the religious traditions of Kalidjaga and Lyusi are accessible, and indeed attractive, to them, the certitude those traditions produced is not. The transformation of religious symbols from imagistic revelations of the divine, evidences of God, to ideological assertions of the divine's importance, badges of piety, has been in each country, though in different ways, the common reaction to this disheartening discovery. And it is this process, as well as the loss of spiritual self-confidence that underlies it, that we need somehow to explain.

As we can hardly trace the entire texture of historical change in recent times for our two countries, let us focus on three separable, but of course hardly unrelated, developments, whose impact upon classical culture has been the most profound: the establishment of Western domination; the increasing influence of scholastic, legalistic, and doctrinal, that is to say, scriptural, Islam; and the crystallization of an activist nation-state. Together these three processes, none of them yet concluded, shook the old order in Indonesia and Morocco as thoroughly, if not so far as productively, as Capitalism, Protestantism, and Nationalism shook it in the West.

If one looks at the colonial periods of the two societies, the first thing that strikes one is the apparently very much greater length of the Indonesian as against the Moroccan. The Indonesian tends to be dated from the founding of Batavia in 1619, the Moroccan from the establishment of the French Protectorate in 1912. But these dates are extremely misleading, the Indonesian because it is much too old, the Moroccan because it is much too recent. Intensive Dutch influence in Indonesia was largely confined to the coastal areas of Java and certain parts of the Moluccas until well into the eighteenth century, and even then control was limited and uneven. On the other hand, forceful European intrusion into the coastal areas of Morocco dates back to the fifteenth century, and from the seventeenth the political and economic intrigues of European powers were a constant element in the Moroccan scene. Without attempting to deny that the intensity of the colonial experience of the two countries differed at all, I think it possible to argue that the most reasonable date for the beginning of high imperialism, the sort whose social effects were lasting and fundamental, is the same in each case: 1830—the year the French took Algiers and the Dutch launched the massive forced cultivation program in Java known, somewhat confusingly, as "The Culture System."

The primary impact of colonialism was, here as elsewhere, economic. The European demand for consumption goods—coffee and sugar in Indonesia, wool and wheat in Morocco—got the period of all-out colonialism under way; the European demand for industrial raw materials—rubber in Indonesia, phosphates in Morocco—consummated it. In between, the foundations of a modern economy, an enclave economy, of course, but a modern one nonetheless, were laid down. One need not quote the figures, which are well enough known, nor rehearse the polemics, which are even better known. The grand monuments of colonialism are not cathedrals, theaters, or palaces, but roads, railways, ports, and banks.

But of course, beyond its economic impact, and largely because of it, colonialism also created a unique, not to say bizarre, political situation. It was not just that the indigenous rulers were either removed or reduced to agents of foreign powers, but, more importantly, that the symbols of legitimacy, the loci of power, and the instruments of authority were rudely dissociated. I have already alluded to this for the Indonesian case: how, after the reduction of Mataram, the Dutch determined, and when need be physically enforced, policy; the transformed aristocracy did most of the day-to-day administrating; and the old courts conserved the illusion of cultural continuity, or anyway tried to. But the same thing is true in Morocco, where the French (and Spanish) governed through the agency of indigenous strong men in the name of the Sherifian Sultanate. The main result of this odd state of affairs was twofold: a framework for national integration of a sort which had not previously existed was created; and the distinction between ruler and ruled became more than a difference in power, status, or situation, it became a difference in cultural identity. At the same time as the Protectorates and the East Indies brought Morocco and Indonesia into being as integrated states, they brought them into being as bifurcated polities.

Bifurcated societies, actually, for around the core of soldiers and colonial officials were collected the plantation managers, commercial farmers, bankers, mine operators, exporters, and merchants (plus, as envoys of conscience, a few clerics, teachers, and savants) for whom the whole enterprise was designed. Hermetic, privileged, and above all foreign, this group formed, as it wished and as it turned out, an indigestible element in each society. No colonial ideology seeking to justify imperialism by removing it to higher ground—neither the *mission civilisatrice* of the culture-vain French, nor the *ethische richting* of the Calvinist Dutch—could ever change this fact. Indeed, these apologia were responses to its stubbornness. Beyond the economic and political, the colonial confrontation was spiritual: a clash of selves. And in this part of the struggle, the colonized, not without cost and not without exception, triumphed: they remained, somewhat made over, themselves.

In this determined maintenance of social personality religion played, as might be expected, a pivotal role. The only thing the colonial elite was not and, a few ambiguous cases aside, could not become was Muslim. The trappings of local culture could be taken on—couscous, burnouses, and moorish arches in Morocco; rijstaffel, sarongs, and wall-less drawing rooms in Indonesia. Local etiquette might be affected, local craftwork cultivated. Even the language might be learned. But it was all *Mauresque* or *Indische*, not Moroccan or Indonesian. The real line between, in the Moroccan phrasing, Nazarenes and Believers, or, in the Indonesian, Christian Men and Islamic Men, was not effaced. Indeed, it grew sharper. In a curiously ironical way, intense involvement with the West moved religious faith closer to the center of our peoples' self-definition than it had been before. Before, men had been Muslims as a matter of circumstance; now they were, increasingly, Muslims as a matter of policy. They were *oppositional* Muslims. Not only oppositional, of course; but into what had been a fine medieval contempt for infidels crept a tense modern note of anxious envy and defensive pride.

But if colonialism created the conditions in which an oppositional, identity-preserving, willed Islam could and did flourish, scripturalism—the turn toward the Koran, the Hadith, and the Sharia, together with various standard commentaries upon them, as the only acceptable bases of religious authority—provided the content of such an Islam. Western intrusion produced a reaction not only against Christianity (that aspect of the matter can easily be overemphasized) but against the classical religious traditions of the two countries themselves. It was not European beliefs and practices, whose impingement on either Moroccan or Indonesian spiritual life was tangential and indirect, toward which the doctrinal fire of the scripturalists was mainly directed; it was maraboutism and illuminationism. Externally stimulated, the upheaval was internal.

In Indonesia, the general movement toward an Islam of the book rather than of the trance or the miracle has commonly been associated with the word *santri*, the Javanese term for a religious student. In Morocco, it has not had any single name, and indeed has been a rather less capsular development, but it has centered around the same figure, there called a *tāleb*. Neither of these movements was highly organized or integrated, indeed, until recently they were hardly organized or integrated at all. Nor was

either of them new in the colonial period: there were bent scholastics disputing in the airless mosque schools of Fez and Demak
almost from the time of Islam's arrival. But it was in the colonial
period, the high colonial period, that they gathered strength and,
culminating, as we shall see, in a kind of convulsive self-purification, threatened for awhile to drive the classical traditions not
merely from the center of the stage but from the scene altogether.

I have already mentioned how, after the implantation of Islam,
Indonesian religious orientations began to sort out into three separate, rather incommensurable streams. The Indic tradition continued, stripped (except in Bali, which was never Islamized) of
the bulk of its ritual expression but not of its inward temper. Its
main strength was on Java and among the privileged classes, but
it was not without representation elsewhere as well. The mass of
the peasantry remained devoted to local spirits, domestic rituals,
and familiar charms. What the particular spirits, rituals, and
charms were differed from group to group, almost from village
to village. But, excepting the Papuan tribes in New Guinea and
the Moluccas, there was and is a family resemblance among them
all, stemming doubtless from a general commonality of ances-
tral forms, what is sometimes called the Malay substratum. Chris-
tians and pagans (about six percent of the population) apart, all
these people, gentry and peasantry alike, conceived themselves to
be Muslims. It was only in the third stream, however, the santri,
that this conception was taken to imply detailed adherence to the
legal, moral, and ritual demands of Islamic scripture. As a confes-
sion, Islam was virtually universal in Indonesia by the end of the
nineteenth century; but as a body of even sporadically observed
canonical doctrine, it was not. Orthodox Islam, or more accurately
Islam which strove to be orthodox, was (and still is) a minority
creed.

The foundations of a more precisian Islam were, as I say, laid
well before the nineteenth century. The brief cross and crescent
florescences in the seventeenth century of Atjeh at the northern
tip of Sumatra, Makassar at the southern tip of the Celebes, and

Bantam at the western tip of Java at least foreshadowed it, as, in a kind of reverse-image way, did the sharpening literary attacks by court poets upon mosque officials and Koranic judges in the eighteenth. But it was only in the nineteenth that it definitively arrived to crystallize into an aggressive counter-tradition, one which indicted as ungodly not only Dutch rule but gentry Indicism and peasant syncretism as well.

The immediate agents of this crystallization were the pilgrimage to Mecca, the Muslim boarding school, and the internal market system. They were not new either, but each grew enormously in importance after 1850, when steamships, trains, and the Suez Canal suddenly shrank the world to domestic dimensions. The pilgrimage, on which some two thousand Indonesians were departing by 1860, ten thousand by 1880, and fifty thousand by 1926, created a new class of spiritual adepts: men who had been to the Holy Land and (so they thought) seen Islam through an undarkened glass. Upon their return the more earnest of them founded religious boarding schools, many of them quite large, to instruct young men in what they took to be the true and neglected teaching of the Prophet. Called either *ulama,* from the Arabic term for religious scholars, or *kijaji,* from the Javanese for sage, these men became the leaders of the santri community, a community which soon expanded to include anyone who had been in a religious school at any time in his life or who even sympathized with the sentiments fostered by such schools whether he had in fact been in one or not.

The connections, in turn, between this, in the Indonesian context, sectarian community and the internal marketing system, a network of small, open-air bazaars, are partly historical and partly functional—historical in that, as I have already noted several times, Islam was drawn to Indonesia by a trade expansion which two centuries later was turned inward by Dutch dominance along the coasts; functional in that there was an elective affinity, to use Weber's famous phrase from Goethe, between itinerant, small-scale, catch-as-catch-can trading and an assortment of informal, independent, freely accessible, virtually costless religious hostels scattered broadly over the countryside. Mosque and market have been a natural pair over much of the Islamic world, paving one another's way in the spread of a civilization interested equally in this world and the next. In Indonesia, where high culture was basically Indic, they emerged, welded together by the pilgrimage and the religious school, as an intrusive, dissonant, destabilizing force.

The forming community of pilgrims, scholars, students, and peddlers first gradually, then with accelerating speed, developed a conception of religiousness in which the illuminationism of the classical style found a progressively smaller and ultimately nonexistent place. In the first phases, the difference between the two traditions was slight; the teachings in the santri schools were hardly more than essentially pre-Islamic beliefs decked out with bits of terminology, pieces of magic, and scraps of imagery picked up from sufi sheikhs in the Holy Land. But as the century wore on, the content of the teaching became not only un-Indic and un-Malaysian, but anti-Indic and anti-Malaysian.

It also became anti-Dutch, and between 1820 and 1880 at least four major (and a multitude of minor) santri insurrections, directed simultaneously against the established traditions and the colonial power, erupted. In West Sumatra in 1821–28, a band of pilgrim zealots, outraged by the heterodoxy of local customs and bent on the establishment of theocratic government, massacred the Indicized royal family and a large number of village officials and were only checked finally by a Dutch military invasion. In Central Java in 1826–30, a disappointed claimant to the Javanese throne proclaimed himself the Mahdi (that is, the Muslim Messiah) and launched a full-scale Holy War against the colonial government and its native agents. In Northwest Java in the 1840s and 1880s, popular outbursts incited by local ulamas wiped out nearly the whole of the resident European community and most of the important Javanese civil servants. In North Sumatra in 1873–1903, the Atjehnese, combining memories of a corsair past, a general contempt for foreigners of all varieties, and a conception of themselves as the keenest Muslims in Asia, embroiled the Dutch in battle for thirty years. By 1900, santri-ism was firmly in being as both a dissident religious ideology and a rebellious political one. And the spiritual balance of power which, as I mentioned in the last chapter, had kept the Indic, the Islamic, and the tree-god minded, if not exactly integrated, at least out of one another's way, was definitively and, so far as I can see, irretrievably lost.

In this century the scripturalist movement proceeded to what, in the nature of the case, was its logical conclusion: radical and uncompromising purism. The rise throughout the Muslim world after 1880 of what has been called, rather vaguely and unsatisfactorily, Islamic Reform—the attempt to reestablish the "plain," "original," "uncorrupted," "progressive" Islam of the Days of the Prophet and the Rightly Guided Caliphs—merely provided an explicit theological base for what, a good deal less reflectively, had been developing in Indonesia for at least half a century. Propagation of the arguments of Middle Eastern back-to-the-Koran and on-to-modernity revivalists like Jamal Ad-Din Al-Afghani or Muhammed Abduh (which by the 1920s was very extensive) did not so much change the direction of santri thought as complete it.

This tense intermixture of radical fundamentalism and determined modernism is what has made the culminating phases of the scripturalist movement so puzzling to Western observers. Stepping backward in order better to leap is an established principle in cultural change; our own Reformation was made that way. But in the Islamic case the stepping backward seems often to have been taken for the leap itself, and what began as a rediscovery of the scriptures ended as a kind of deification of them. "The Declaration of the Rights of Man, the secret of atomic power, and the principles of scientific medicine," an advanced kijaji once informed me, "are all to be found in the Koran," and he proceeded to quote what he regarded as the relevant passages. Islam, in this way, becomes a justification for modernity, without itself actually becoming modern. It promotes what it itself, to speak metaphorically, can neither embrace nor understand. Rather than the first stages in Islam's reformation, scripturalism in this century has come, in both Indonesia and Morocco, to represent the last stages in its ideologization.

Though in its broad outlines the Moroccan movement toward a schoolmaster's Islam was astonishingly similar to the Indonesian, the way in which it worked out in detail and the particular manner in which it exercised its impact were somewhat different. There are a number of reasons for this. In the first place, though both societies had something of a scholarly tradition in the properly Islamic sense from the beginning, the Moroccan was much more developed than the Indonesian, where, with a few exceptions, the accomplished poets, chroniclers, and philosophers were Indic in outlook and training. Second, and perhaps even more important, Arabic was the mother tongue of at least a large part of the population in Morocco (and a closely related one for the rest), whereas in Indonesia it was a foreign language, a very foreign language, which even among the ulamas and kijajis probably not one person in a hundred ever really mastered. Arabism thus played a role in the scripturalist defense of national personality in Morocco that was not possible in Indonesia, where the santris chanted their Koran in echoed accents and gained what understanding of the text they might from vernacular summaries and annotations dictated by teachers whose grasp of the original was in most cases not much greater than their own. Indonesians could be, and in spurts were, pan-Islamicists, but they could not quite be pan-Arabists; Moroccans could be both, and indeed did not distinguish between them.

And finally, the Moroccans had, in the days of Granada, Seville, and Cordoba, been on the immediate peripheries, at least, of a great Islamic civilization—some would say the greatest—while the Indonesians had never been anywhere near any of the major florescences of Muslim culture. Even the Mughal, which was the closest, seems hardly to have touched them. To have had a direct contact with centers of sophisticated thought, as to a degree Morocco did before the fourteenth century, and then to have lost it is a quite different matter than never really to have had it at all. It is easier to revive one's own past, even one's imagined past, than to import someone else's and revive that.

Yet despite all this, it would be a mistake to rate the Moroccan scholarly tradition very highly. It was always a confined and specialized thing, a matter of a few withdrawn pedants, of whom the early eighteenth century figure who managed to give twenty-one hundred lectures (to what audience it is not reported) on the subject of the particle "b–" in the expression *bismi'llah* is, though a caricature, a perhaps not altogether misleading example. As a popular movement, scripturalism is no older in Morocco than in Indonesia and, at least so far as I can see, not all that more learned. It is, however, much more endogenously rooted, much more of an autochthonous growth.

Here scripturalism, for all its opposition to maraboutism, came not as an intrusive force disrupting a delicate balance among incompatible commitments, but as a continuation of the centuries' long trend toward spiritual consolidation. As the sherifian principle, the genealogization of charisma, had brought saint worship, the brotherhoods, and the royal cult within a single, if loose, framework of hereditary maraboutism, so the scripturalist movement attempted to replace this synthesis, which it regarded as heretical and outworn, with one based on credal orthodoxy exactly defined. The struggle between the champions of the older pattern and those of the new was bitter and intense, and it has not ended yet. But it was a struggle for religious leadership of the whole nation, not merely of a part of it. The rise of scripturalism did not lead, as it did in Indonesia, toward spiritual partition, the hardening of accepted variations into absolute divisions; it led toward spiritual focalization, the confinement of religious life within a narrower, more sharply demarcated circle.

The vehicle of this focalization was again the so-called "reform," or "fundamentalist" or "modernist" or "neo-orthodox"

movement founded at the end of the nineteenth century by the
Egyptian theologian Muhammed Abduh, and usually known in
Arabic as the Salafi movement, from *as-salāf as-ṣāliḥ*, literally
"the righteous ancestors"—Muhammed and his Companions.
Here too the groundwork was laid earlier, mainly by scholars
around the Sultanate and in the famous mosque university in
Fez, the Qarawiyyin. Open attacks on maraboutism began as
early as the turn of the eighteenth century. But it was not until
the 1870s, when a Moroccan—another restless Berber in from
the hinterlands, in fact—returned from studying in Egypt to ad-
vocate, in the Qarawiyyin and in the royal council of scholars, a
literalist interpretation of the scriptures, a discarding of post-Ko-
ranic commentaries, and a rejection of Sufism in all its forms,
that Salafi ideas began, even in restricted circles, really to take
hold. By 1900 the battle between scripturalism and maraboutism
was definitely joined. By the 1920s, it dominated not just scholarly discussion but popular as well, and the boast of Allal Al-
Fassi, ultimately the movement's leading personality, that "the
manner in which the Salafi movement [was] conducted in Morocco . . . secured for it a degree of success unequalled even in
the country of Muhammad Abduh and Jamal al-Din, where it
originated" was a far from idle one. Actually, despite the limita-
tion of Salafism (not, in any case, there called that) to but a sub-
group of the population, it would not have been an idle one for
Indonesia either.

As in Indonesia, the first expressions of the scripturalist impulse were tentative and still not sharply set apart from the general drift of established practice. Sultans collected anti-sufis
around them as they collected sufis, anti-legists as they collected
legists, reformers as they collected anti-reformers, playing them
off against one another and attempting to keep them all centered
on his, the Sultan's, person as the First Muslim of the country.
Among the general populace, the spread of organized religious
schools was once more the main agency of scripturalist penetration, only here the masters of such schools were not returned pilgrims but merely Marrakech, Rabat, Tetuan, or, especially, Fez

educated petty scholastics called talebs. Mostly they taught children to chant and copy the Koran as well as attempting to impart to the older and brighter ones something of the general outlines of Islamic law. Supported, barely, by pious foundations and personal contributions from their students' parents, these "porters of the Koran," as the French called them, lived the mean and lonely life of a wandering medieval tutor. Most of them were landless exiles from their home areas, pushed out by poverty to earn their keep as religious specialists, much as younger peasant sons were once sent off into the lower clergy in Europe. Delivering their message in every setting from city cubicles to tribal tents, often moving after three or four years from one camp, village, or town to the next, they were at once formally respected as learned and informally despised as menials. Most of them knew little, and much of that was wrong. They trafficked in amulets and dabbled in sorcery. But in the course of the nineteenth century, they spread over much of the country and taught thousands of ordinary Moroccans to read a certain amount of Arabic, perform a certain amount of ritual, and above all to regard the Koran not merely as a fetish radiating baraka but as a body of precepts to be memorized, comprehended, and observed.

That more was memorized than comprehended, and more comprehended than observed is only to be expected. But the ground for Salafi purism was at least prepared. And through Salafi purism the ground for nationalism was at least prepared. In both Indonesia and Morocco the prologue to nationalism coincides with the epilogue to scripturalism. The first mass nationalist organizations—the 1912 Sarekat Islam (The Islamic Union) in Indonesia and the 1930 Kutlat al-'Amal al-Watani (The National Action Bloc) in Morocco—were immediate products of the scripturalist movement, expressions as much of the impulse to religious self-purification as to political self-assertion. Indeed, the two were so closely entwined as to be almost indistinguishable. But the alliance did not last. The fusion was a temporary one. And in the end, that is to say, after independence, the scripturalists found themselves politically disinherited, progressively isolated from the by now rapidly expanding machinery of state power. The strategy of embracing the twentieth century by reincarnating the seventh did not in the end work out very well. Men whose religious commitments were more traditional and whose political ones were less came to dominate the nationalist movements and, when those movements succeeded, the nations they created.

Seeing history in terms of personalities, especially dramatic personalities, is always dangerous; it is not *virtus* which moves society. Yet that the history of our two countries from the late 1920s to the early 1960s, those three or four decades in which almost everything that could conceivably have happened did happen, is inextricably entangled with the careers of on the one hand Sukarno and on the other Muhammed V, is beyond any question. If they did not wholly make the history of their times— and they made a good deal of it—they surely embodied it. Like Kalidjaga and Lyusi, they sum up much more than they ever were.

And what they sum up is not so very different from what the classical figures summed up as the radically dissimilar historical situation in which they operated (and thus, the radically dissimilar results which flowed from their actions) might make it appear. Sukarno and Muhammed V coped with a political, economic, and cultural transition both vaster and more drastic than those which followed the collapse of Madjapahit and the end of High Barbary; but they coped with it, each of them, in a style more than a little familiar. With Sukarno the theater state returned to Indonesia; and with Muhammed V maraboutic kingship returned to Morocco.

The impact of these two momentous personalities was, of course, largely exercised through the political roles they ultimately came to occupy: the Indonesian Presidency and the Moroccan Sultanate. The Presidency was, it is true, a newly created institution, created indeed by Sukarno virtually single-handedly, while the Sultanate was a venerable institution by the time Muhammed V became the twenty-second Alawite sovereign. Yet as in the case of the lengths of the colonial periods, the differences can easily be exaggerated. Muhammed V made, in his quiet, tenacious, blandly recalcitrant way, a radically new thing out of the Sultanate. A museum piece when its French "protectors" awarded it to him in 1927, his impact upon it was at least as great as its impact upon him, and when he died in 1961 he left it a revived and transformed office. On the other hand, there is about Sukarno's conception of the Presidency, that so Western-looking invention, something, as a number of people have pointed out, of the quality of the Mataram kingship. It is not so easy as it appears to tell who is chief executive and who is monarch here. In fact, neither role was simply new or simply old, neither man simply revolutionary or simply traditional. They were like those trick cartoons I used to see as a child which, turned one way, showed a bald, wrinkled old man with a long beard and a thoughtful brow; turned the other, a beardless, round-eyed youth with a wild head of hair and a witless grin. The states the two roles crowned and the two men ruled are like that too; which is at least part of the reason why the reports on their nature have been so contradictory.

The Moroccan monarchy, to begin with it, is not just the key institution in the Moroccan political system. That, one would naturally expect. It is also, as I suggested in the last chapter, the key institution in the Moroccan religious system, which is perhaps a bit more surprising, at least in the middle of the twentieth century. Not only that, but even within the Islamic world, where one is accustomed to a certain difficulty in separating God's things from Caesar's, the Moroccan monarchy is a distinctly peculiar institution.

At the most fundamental level this peculiarity stems from the fact that the monarchy combines within itself what are probably the two major traditions of political legitimacy in Islam, traditions which, on the face of it, would seem, like The Divine Right of Kings and The Doctrine of the General Will (which, in fact, they distantly resemble), to be radically and irreconcilably opposed. In most places, they have been; but in Morocco, where the talent for forcing things together which really do not go together is rather highly developed, they are fused if not exactly into a seamless whole at least into an integral institution which has, so far, proved quite effective in containing, even in capitalizing on, its own inner contradictions.

The two traditions, or concepts, of legitimacy are those called by W. Montgomery Watt, the Edinburgh Islamicist, the "autocratic" and the "constitutionalist." But as what is involved is not tyranny vs. democracy, or even arbitrariness vs. legalism, but whether authority is conceived to emanate from a charismatic individual or from a charismatic community, I find these terms misleading and will use instead the "intrinsic" and the "contractual." As Watt says, the critical question is whether the right to rule is seen as an organic property magically ingredient in the ruler's person or as conferred upon him, in some occult and complicated way, by the population he rules. And in Morocco the answer to this question is "both."

The "intrinsic" theory of legitimacy, the one which sees authority inherent in the ruler as ruler, traces back, in Watt's view, to the Shia notion of a sacred leader, the *Imām;* the "contractual" theory he traces to the Sunni concept of a sacred community, the *Umma.* The Imam idea stems, of course, from the Shia recognition, and the Sunni rejection, of the claim of Muhammed's son-in-law Ali and his descendants to an inherited, and heritable, right to the Caliphate, the spiritual leadership of Islamic society. The Umma idea stems from the insistence of Sunni jurists on submission to a standardized interpretation of rite and doctrine—their interpretation—as the defining feature of membership in Muhammed's Community, a submission as binding upon kings as it is upon shepherds. The historical, juridical, and theological problems are very complicated here, involving a host of currents and counter-currents within traditional Islam. But they are not critical for us. What is critical is that, under the Alawites, the Moroccan Sultanate put together what, in most other parts of the Muslim world, were directly antithetical principles of political and religious organization: the principle that the ruler is ruler because he is supernaturally qualified to be so; and the principle that the ruler is ruler because the competent spokesmen of the Community have collectively agreed that he is.

The "intrinsic" dimension of the Sultan's role derived, as I have already explained, from his Prophetic descent, and especially from the fact that he was a close relative, usually a son, occasionally a brother, of the previous Sultan, whose baraka he thus inherited. The "contractual" dimensions rested, however, on an ancient Sunni institution called the *bai'a*, which, deriving from the root "to sell," means a business deal or commercial transaction, and by extension "agreement," "arrangement," or "homage." Until 1962, when Muhammed V introduced one, there was no primo-genitural rule in Morocco, and indeed, aside from the requirement that the Sultan come from the ruling house, no very clear succession rule at all. In fact, most sultans were selected from among the eligibles by their predecessor or by the clique around the throne. But the formal choice, the actual investiture, was carried out by a congress of religious scholars, *'ulema,* sitting in Fez and ratified by similar meetings of scholars and notables in the other major towns. We need not pause here to discuss how far all this was form and how far substance. The point is that the baia in a sense legitimized the Sultan's legitimacy: over the top of his personal charisma it laid the charisma of the Dutiful Community.

This double basis of legitimacy led in turn, or perhaps more accurately, was a result of, a double perception of the nature of the Sultanate among the population. On the one hand, the Sultan was the chief marabout of the country, the ranking saint; his authority was spiritual. On the other hand, the Sultan was the duly chosen leader of the Islamic Community, its officially appointed head; his authority was political. And what is more, these two concepts of what the Sultan was were not equally diffused throughout the society: his sacredness was universally recognized, or virtually so, but his sovereignty most definitely was not. He reigned everywhere, but he ruled only in places.

In the Moroccan idiom this distinction was expressed in terms of the famous, probably too famous, contrast between "the land of government" and "the land of dissidence"—*blad l-makhzen* and *blad s-siba*. Most simply put, the land of government included the regions, largely the towns and villages of the cis-Atlas lowlands, where the population had legally consented, through a baia, to the delegation of supreme governmental powers to the Sultan and, beyond him, to his staff, the Makhzen. Here, there were royal appointed governors, district chiefs, market inspectors, and Koranic judges, as well as royal taxation, royal soldiers, royal justice, and royal domains. In the land of dissidence—mostly the peripheral mountain, desert, and steppe areas—there were no such baias, and so no such governors, chiefs, or judges, but tribal organization plus a greater or lesser respect for the Sultan's person as the religious head of the country, the Imam. It was this odd institution, further tortured out of shape by its adaptation to colonial purposes, to which, at the tender age of seventeen, Muhammed V was suddenly elevated by the French. He received his baia to the strains of the "Marseillaise" just as, a few miles away, scripturalism and nationalism were beginning to forge their uncertain alliance.

As enfeebled, and indeed gutted, as it had been by its subjection to French domination, the Sultanate remained the heart of the Moroccan political and religious system: the prize for which nationalists, scripturalists, Marxists, traditionalists, the French, and, much to the surprise of those who thought him a spoiled and feckless youth, the Sultan himself, bitterly fought. There is probably no other liberated colony in which the struggle for independence so centered around the capture, revival, and renovation of a traditional institution. The decisive phases of nationalism in Morocco (roughly 1930 to 1960) can almost be described as a contest between the scripturalists and the Sultan (and, of course, between both of them and the French) for the Sultanate, for the right to define, or better, redefine it—a contest the Sultan, not entirely through his own doing, rather definitively won. If the Moroccan revolution were to have a slogan beyond that of the banal "freedom!" (*istiqlal!*), it perhaps should be: "The Sultanate is dead; long live the Sultanate!"

The axis of the struggle between, if I may call it so, scripturalist nationalism and royalist nationalism was again the relative emphasis to be placed upon the "intrinsic" and the "contractual" aspects of the Sultanate. Before this century, the community investiture of the Sultan was surely more an acknowledgment of an accomplished fact, an act of homage, than it was a genuine compact. But with the growth of scripturalism, the contract notion began, like so much else regarded as truly Islamic, to be taken rather more literally; the notion of dynastic charisma, like so much else regarded as local heresy, to be openly attacked. The events through which the clash between the partisans of a deputative monarchy and those of a maraboutic one worked itself out are numerous and complex, but two of them define its general course: the issuance, in the Sultan's name, of the so-called Berber Decree in 1930; and the deposition, exile, and return of the Sultan in 1953–55.

The Berber Decree amounted to an attempt by the French to solidify the distinction between the land of government and the land of dissidence and to put the latter under direct French control, unmediated by the Sultanate in even its purely religious aspects. Concretely, it removed the Berbers, most of whom lived in the peripheral regions, from submission to the sharia, the Islamic law, placing them instead under their own customary courts. To a certain extent, this merely legalized an existing state of affairs. But in so doing it also suggested, as it was designed to, that the Berbers were not "really" Muslims, that Koranic law not only had not penetrated very deeply in many of the remoter regions of the country but that it ought not to be allowed to do so, and that the Sultan was not in fact the spiritual head of the whole country after all. It would seem that a policy able to threaten at once maraboutists, scripturalists, royalists, and nationalists and drive them into one another's arms would be difficult to devise;

but with the Berber Decree the French managed to produce one. "It was," as Charles-Andre Julien has said, "more than a juridical crime, it was a political mistake."

Just how big a mistake soon became apparent. The small cliques of nationalist intellectuals in Fez and Rabat suddenly found themselves presented with the cause they had been waiting for and, fusing under the leadership of the zealotic scripturalist, Allal Al-Fassi, launched, in the name of an insulted Islam, the first mass movement for independence—the aforementioned National Action Bloc. Popular demonstrations broke out in the major towns; public prayers invoking divine condemnation upon the French were held all over the country; Al-Fassi and his colleagues harangued huge crowds in the major mosques. The issue, taken up by the pan-Islamic movement, spread even beyond Morocco's borders, and committees to save the Berbers for Islam were set up in Egypt, India, and—the only direct historical connection between our two countries I have been able to discover —Java. This was the high tide of scripturalist nationalism, its climactic moment. If Morocco had become independent in the 1930s, a sheer impossibility, it would doubtless have done so against the monarchy, and Al-Fassi would doubtless have been the Sukarno, the Nkrumah, or the Houphouet of Morocco. As it actually became independent in 1956, it did so through the monarchy, and Al-Fassi was but another attendant politician.

The steady rise of the Sultan's importance within the nationalist movement and the increasingly uneasy relationship it produced between him and the scripturalists can be traced all through the 1930s and 40s as political agitation tended to center more and more about Muhammed V's emerging personality and less and less about the restoration of primordial Islam. But it was his deposition and exile by the French in August of 1953, precipitated by his unwillingness to sign any more prefabricated decrees, that secured for him absolute leadership of it. When, just a little more than two years later, he returned to head an independent Morocco, he was something no Alawite sultan, however powerful, had ever been before, an authentic popular hero. The inscriptions that had

appeared on the banners in the early nationalist demonstrations—
"Long live Islam!" "Long live Morocco!" "Long live the Sultan!"
—were effectively reversed. French rule had produced what, left
to itself, the dynasty was almost certainly no longer capable of
creating—a maraboutic king.

The great peculiarity of this state of affairs needs to be empha-
sized. I doubt that there is any other new nation, if Morocco
really is a new nation, in which the hero-leader of the revolution
and independence was as engulfed in *religious* authority, over
and above the political, as Muhammed V was in Morocco in
1956. If Gandhi rather than Nehru had been India's first Prime
Minister, you perhaps would have had a comparable case, though
the content of both the religious and political convictions of the
two men was of course radically different. It is always difficult to
be sure of such things where the mighty are concerned, but Muhammed V seems actually to have been a man of deep and genuine piety, a piety of a sort more consonant with the personalism
of the classical style than with the dialectics of scripturalism.
Hannah Arendt has remarked that the astonishing thing about
the papacy of John XXIII was that a Christian finally got to be
Pope. In the same way, the astonishing thing about the five short
years of Muhammed V's reign as an independent sovereign is that
a Muslim finally got to be Sultan.

The internal tension between strong man and holy man was
hardly resolved, however. It is irresolvable. Indeed, given the will
to be modern that no new state can live without, the tension is
even greater. Unveiling his daughters but secluding his wives,
wearing Western clothes in private but Arabic robes in public,
rationalizing the governmental bureaucracy but revivifying the
traditional procedures of the court, Muhammed V was a prime
example of the radical disjunction between the forms of religious
life and the substance of secular life I mentioned in the first chapter as characterizing Moroccan Islam today. Muhammed V did
not live long enough to see whether this deliberate segregation
of the spiritual and the practical could endure at such rarefied
heights. His death—sudden, premature, and marked by one of

the greatest collective mourning demonstrations the world has ever seen—merely secured his sainthood that much more certainly. Barring accidents (the last thing one ought to bar in dealing with the Third World), his myth will preside over Morocco's destiny for some time to come. And with it, haunting those who follow him, will preside the image of a man who managed, by sectioning his life into disconnected spheres, to be at once an homme fétiche and an artful politician.

Sukarno's story is at once simpler and more complicated. The son of a Javanese schoolteacher, and thus a member of the lower gentry, he found no established role waiting for him. Javanese courts existed still in Jogjakarta and Surakarta, the remnants of the old Mataram; but they had no political functions at all and were utterly without prospect of achieving any. From the beginning of his career to what appears to be its end, Sukarno was forced to create the institutions he needed as he went. He was an amateur, a parvenu, an eclectic, an autodidact. He played it all by ear.

A born revolutionary, his life reads like a *deuxième bureau* dossier. 1916: boards in the home of H. O. S. Tjokroaminoto, founder of the Islamic Union, the first mass nationalist organization in Indonesia, which he joins. 1925: founds, in Bandung, where he is ostensibly studying to be a civil engineer, a student political club. 1927: transforms the club into the Nationalist Party of Indonesia and becomes its head. 1929: arrested by the Dutch for political activities; publicly tried; imprisoned for two years. 1932: released from jail; elected head of the Nationalist Party, now operating under a new name. 1933: rearrested; exiled without trial to Flores. 1942: freed by the occupying Japanese; placed at the head of a whole series of mass organizations. 1945: proclaims, with Mohammad Hatta, Indonesia's Declaration of Independence; assumes leadership of the revolutionary Republic and the war against the Dutch. 1949: becomes first President of independent Indonesia. 1960: dissolves parliament; bans opposition parties; sets up a presidential autocracy. 1967: replaced, de facto though not officially, as head of state by military takeover; retires to the wings to await either death or another turn of the wheel. Fifty years of agitation, conspiracy, invention, and maneuver; a life of unremitting excitement. "I [am] bound in spiritual longing by the romanticism of revolution," he cries in 1960 as he "buries" what he calls "free-fight liberalism" and "bourgeois democracy." "I am inspired by it. I am fascinated by it. I am completely absorbed by it. I am crazed, I am obsessed by the romanticism of the revolution."

As with most manias, the symptoms set in slowly, but the predisposition was there from the start. From the days at Tjokroaminoto's, where the future leaders of all wings of the nationalist movement—scripturalist, traditionalist, assimilationist, Marxist—met to debate principles and tactics, through the doctrinal infighting of the Revolution, to the desperate sloganizing of "Guided Democracy," Sukarno moved along a rising curve of ideological enthusiasm. His skills, which were enormous, were all rhetorical, even those which were not evinced in words. Where Muhammed V set out quietly, even diffidently, to assert the force inherent in an established institution, he set out brazenly, and hardly silently, to capture the imagination of a people who thought they had seen the last of kings.

The intensely intellectualist character of Indonesian nationalism, its extreme reliance upon what Herbert Feith has called symbol manipulation, has often been noted, but not, I think, as often understood. Sukarno not only had no throne to inherit, he had no comprehensive party organization as, say, Nkrumah had in Ghana, no modernized civil service as Nehru had in India, no populistic army as Nasser had in Egypt. He did not even have the indigenous bourgeoisie upon which Quezon built in the Philippines or the tribal pride upon which Kenyatta built in Kenya. He had only ideology and those men to whom ideology most appeals—the intelligentsia. The role of the intellectual, that unreliable figure Réal de Curban defined as a man with more Latin than property (though here, the language was Dutch), was as great in Indonesian nationalism as in that of any other new state, save, perhaps, Algeria. Burkhardt's terrible simplifiers found their Erewhon in Indonesia, and it was Sukarno, with more lives than a cat and more nerve than a burglar, who, at virtually every crucial juncture, provided them with the necessary simplifications.

Simplifying simplifications is not an inviting task. But there were, in Sukarno's and Indonesia's progress toward what he himself has called a *mythos*, three major ideological phases—the first centered around his Colonial Period agitation; the second centered around the Revolution; and the third centered around the period of presidential autocracy. Being phases, and growing out of one another, the later ones do not replace the earlier ones but merely engulf them in an expanding complex of symbols. But they mark, nonetheless, reasonably distinct steps in the advance toward the re-creation of a theater state, the revival, in the face of both the scripturalist and the Marxist brands of purism, of exemplary politics.

The Colonial Period phase consisted largely of trying to get free of scripturalism and Marxism and forge a "genuinely Indonesian" creed. After the Islamic Union split in 1921 into its scripturalist and Marxist wings—the latter evolving shortly thereafter into the Indonesian Communist Party—Sukarno moved, in setting up the Nationalist Party, to establish such a creed. Called "Marhaenism," after the name of a poor peasant Sukarno claims to have met and talked with one day while strolling through the rice terraces during the late 1920s, it rested on a distinction between the small peasant, market seller, artisan, cart driver, and so on, who owns his own land, tools, horse, or whatever, that is to say, is propertied, but who is yet impoverished, and the true proletarian in the Marxist sense, who sells his labor power without participating in the means of production. Indonesia was a society of men like the peasant, Marhaen; colonialism had, as he said in his famous defense before the Bandung court in 1929, made everything and everyone small—the farmer, the worker, the trader, the clerk, all came to have "the stamp of smallness." As a doctrine, Marhaenism was mere primitive populism, a mass-action mystique, and it never became anything more than that. But with it Sukarno relieved himself from, as he once put it, the necessity of waiting for salvation by an airplane from Moscow or a Caliph from Istanbul.

Others, however, kept on waiting, and by the time of the Revolution the contention among the leading political camps—Islamic, Marxist, and Populist—was extraordinarily intense. Sukarno's next ideological invention was consequently an attempt at synthesis. In the so-called *Pantjasila* (The Five points), first set forth in 1945 as a creed for the coming Republic, he sought to lay the foundations for Revolutionary unity by restoring the sort of spiritual balance of power that the events of the previous hundred, and especially the previous twenty, years had destroyed. There was in the Five Points—Nationalism, Humanitarianism, Democracy, Social Justice, and Belief in God—something for everyone, suitably distributed. Or at least Sukarno devoutly hoped that there was. For he saw himself as the exemplar of this sort of eclectic integration an ideological microcosm: "I am a follower of Karl Marx," he announced once in a speech, "but, on the other hand, I am also a religious man, so I can grasp the entire gamut between Marxism and theism. . . . I know all the trends and understand them. . . . I have made myself the meeting place of all trends and ideologies. I have blended, blended, and blended them until finally they became the present Sukarno."

As is generally known, things did not work themselves out as harmoniously in the society at large; the world around did not automatically shape itself in the image of its exemplary leader. By 1957, and indeed before then, the contrast between the cosmos pictured in the Pantjasila and embodied in Sukarno and the chaos obtaining in daily life was great enough for even the most adoring courtier to notice. The third of Sukarno's ideological contrivances, the one which, when it too failed, destroyed him, consisted of an attempt to bring the two into line, not by changing the ideal, which was sacred, nor yet by enforcing it, which was beyond his powers, but by "re-shaping" (the word, used in English, is his own) the political institutions and with them the political morality of the national government to more faithfully reflect it. He called this "Guided Democracy," but what he created, or tried to create, was a modern version of the theater state, a state from whose pageants, myths, celebrities, and monuments the small peasant or peddler, the enduring Marhaen, could derive a vision of his nation's greatness and strive to realize it.

There is no need to describe here in any detail the ingredients of this climactic surge of exemplary politics—the building of the world's largest mosque, a colossal sports stadium, and a national monument higher than the Eiffel Tower, larger than Borobodur, and designed to last a thousand years; the circus ceremonialism of Asian Games, New Life Movements, New Guinea crusades, and Malaysian Confrontations; the Kafkaesque labyrinth of Supreme Advisory Councils, National Planning Boards, forty-member Cabinets, and Temporary Consultative Assemblies, topped by a life-term Presidency. All this, together with the flood of acronyms, slogans, catchwords, and proclamations which surrounded it, has been discussed at great length, if not always with equivalent depth, in the recent literature on Indonesia. The point, so far as we are concerned, is that after 1960 the doctrine that the welfare of a country proceeds from the excellence of its capital, the excellence of its capital from the brilliance of its elite, and the brilliance of its elite from the spirituality of its ruler reemerged in full force in Indonesia.

Yet it is necessary to be clear here. The new exemplarism did not emerge out of Indonesia's collective unconscious, it was not a return of the culturally repressed. Sukarno, less plebian than he imagined and less radical than he sounded, was the historical heir of the Indic tradition as surely as Muhammed V was the heir to the sherifian Sultanate. This tradition had been maintained, as I explained earlier, by the bureaucratized gentry of the Colonial Period. And it was from this class—or, more accurately, the lower, revolutionary edge of it—that Sukarno emerged and to which, for all his attacks on "feudalism," he never ceased to belong, for which he never ceased to speak. Its religious style was his own and so, readjusted to modern conditions and purged of colonial submissiveness, were its ideals. In his expansive, world-embracing manner he once told Louis Fisher that he was simultaneously a Christian, a Muslim, and a Hindu. But it was the shadow-play stories from the Ramayana and Mahabharata that he knew by heart, not the Bible or the Koran; and it was in self-communion, not in churches or mosques, that he looked for divine guidance. Sukarno, too, had his moment by the riverside, and if we are to believe him, which in this instance we would, I think, be well advised to do, what happened to him there was, one imagines, about what happened to Kalidjaga in Djapara:

> When I recall the five years of my life in Flores, how, as I sat on the shore at sundown . . . I listened to the wild roar of the waves dashing upon the beach, and as I sat alone, lost in thought on that Flores shore, I heard the sea chanting a song of praise to God Almighty: "Oh God, my Lord, you have given our people such beauty as this." If I recall when I was in Bengkulu [a town in southwest Sumatra, where he was confined after being moved from Flores], I would often leave the town and enter the jungle; the breeze would rustle softly through the trees, leaves would fall to earth. That wind . . . rustling softly in the forest, that wind, to my ears, was singing soft praises, Indonesia's praises, to the Almighty.

In any case, the hero leaders are gone now. Muhammed V died, after what was supposed to be a routine nasal operation but apparently was something more, in 1961. Sukarno, after his cardboard Mataram collapsed in an enormous pool of blood, was at last removed from power in March of 1967. They are hard acts to follow, not only because they were, in their time, such popular figures, but because they communicated to their peoples such an overwhelming sense of promise, a promise their less colorful successors, Hassan II and General Suharto, must somehow contrive to redeem.

Just what the future of religion in general and Islam in particular in the two countries is, is unclear. Scripturalism remains a powerful force in both and indeed seems at the moment to be gaining ground once more. Political ground, that is, for religious rethinking is, if anything, even less in evidence than it was in the Nationalist Period. Nothing has been done since Abduh, nothing seems (though one can never be sure) likely to be done, and scripturalism seems likely to remain in the position of cheering on a modernism whose every advance undermines its own position. Or perhaps a reaction will set in, and the powerful anti-modern forces which are also contained in scripturalism, the fundamentalist side of it, come to the fore. There are already some signs of this, too, in both countries, and especially in Morocco.

As for Marxism, which, whatever temporary alliances it may make with religion, is ultimately a secularizing force, it seems at the moment in retreat in both countries. Never very powerful in Morocco, it is under intense attack by the government. In Indonesia the coup and the slaughter, mostly of communist sympathizers (or suspected such), which followed it has clearly halted its forward thrust there. In both cases the arrest is almost certainly not permanent, and as a spiritual force, as well as a political one, Marxism will be heard from again in both countries.

But despite the death of Muhammed V and the deposition of Sukarno, the classical styles they carried forth and renovated are still the axial traditions. Hassan II, his power resting almost entirely on the legitimacy of the Sultanate in the eyes of the masses, has striven to keep the image of his father as a monarch-saint, a fusion of holy man and strong man, alive, and, less successfully, to merge his own image with it. General Suharto, lacking Sukarno's self-dramatizing gifts, is still himself both Indically inclined and concerned to reestablish some sort of spiritual balance of power in Indonesia, if only so as to be able to rule. And, indeed, the so-called "New Order" in Indonesia is already beginning to evince some of the traits of Sukarno-like theatricalism.

Predictions in this field, however, are pointless. All a student of comparative religion can really do is to lay out the general limits within which the spiritual life of a people has moved, is moving, and, the future never being wholly unlike the present, is likely to go on moving. Just how, within those general limits, it will in fact move, God, as they say, only knows.

4. The Struggle for the Real

Some three or four decades ago, in that digressive paren-
thesis between the wars when Western thought wandered down
so many crooked ways, there raged in anthropology something
of a great debate concerning what went on in the heads of savages. As in most such debates, the main participants were too
busy talking to listen carefully, so that not only did they not understand one another very well but they were inclined to advance
their arguments by denying propositions no one had in fact asserted. And like most such debates, it eventually expired more
because people grew bored with it and moved on to other things
than because it came to any definitive resolution. Yet it was, we
can now see, the beginning, within anthropology at least, of
something important: the conception of human culture as consisting not so much in customs and institutions as in the sorts of
interpretations the members of a soceity apply to their experience,
the constructions they put upon the events through which they
live; not just how people behave, but how they look at things.

Almost all anthropologists of any note contributed to this discussion of what unfortunately came to be known as the "primitive thought" problem; but perhaps the two most significant,
particularly if significance is measured by the ability to infuriate
others, were the Polish-English ethnographer Bronislaw Malinowski and the French philosopher Lucien Lévy-Bruhl. Whether
they intended to or not, these two men came to stand for the extreme positions in the debate: in Malinowski's case, primitive
pragmatism; in Lévy-Bruhl's, primitive mysticism. The dispute
came down to, or anyway was made to come down to, the question of whether "savages" (as we then were free to call them)

viewed the world in an essentially commonsensical way, as a field of practical problems demanding practical solutions, or in an essentially affective way, as a series of emotional encounters demanding emotional responses.

To state the issue in so undressed a form is to expose its unreality; the conclusion that the dichotomy is a false one and that any man, civilized or not, is prudent and passionate by turns arises virtually of itself. And at length this was indeed the conclusion that was generally drawn, even by the protagonists themselves, who adjusted their polemics accordingly. But compromises, even reasonable compromises, are not always so advantageous in science as they are in politics, and in this case the "there is something to be said for both sides" position merely conduced to a wholesale missing of the point.

For the important question the "primitive thought" debate raised was not whether savages are rational or not, or even whether their mental processes differ from ours or not. They are and they aren't; they do and they don't. The important question the debate raised, and then proceeded promptly to obscure, was, "What are the differences between a commonsense orientation to the world and a religious one, and what are the relations between them?" What was taken to be an investigation of the "savage mind" was in fact an investigation of the varieties of human understanding, of the diverse ways in which men, all men, attempt to render their lives intelligible by ordering the separate events in which they find themselves caught up into connected patterns of experience.

"A moment's reflection is sufficient," Malinowski wrote on the very first page of his most important theoretical work, *Magic, Science and Religion*, "to show that no art or craft, however primitive, could have been invented or maintained, no organized form of hunting, fishing, tilling, or search for food, could be carried out without the careful observation of natural process and a firm belief in its regularity, without the power of reasoning and without confidence in the power of reason." A moment's reflection is indeed sufficient to show this, a fact which leads one to wonder whether anyone sane has ever denied it. But it is not sufficient to demonstrate the validity of the proposition Malinowski regarded as a corollary of this truism, namely that all aspects of human activity are governed by this same spirit of sensible practicality.

Though coated in a veneer of emotion and mysticism, magic, myth, and ritual are, in his view, all instrumental activities at base. Magic, founded on the conviction that "hope cannot fail nor desire deceive," sustains action in situations where reliable knowledge is weak or lacking. The savage can make reasonably sure that his canoe will not sink from poor construction, but not that it won't be destroyed, and he with it, in a storm; so against the latter he invokes his compulsive spells. Myth buttresses established social institutions by providing them with a quasi-historical charter which explains and justifies them, a sacred constitution, as it were. Ritual sustains general morale, especially in times of stress, by asserting and demonstrating the interdependence among men, the adaptational necessity of social life. Even the most other-worldly-looking practices are thus means of coping with quite down-to-earth problems: getting up the nerve to put to sea in an open boat; maintaining composure at a funeral; revivifying the ties that bind, the sentimental attachments among kinsmen.

This view is not wholly without truth. Ritual, magic, myth do without doubt serve in these mundane ways, and more than one person has been attracted or held to religion in the hope, not always vain, of improving his health, raising his status, or advancing his fortunes. Whole priesthoods have been recruited that way. But there is also little doubt that a thoroughgoing instrumentalist view of such phenomena reduces them to caricatures of themselves by leaving out of account that which most sets them apart as distinctive forms of life. When Malinowski concludes that religion has an immense biological value because it enhances "practical mental attitudes," because it reveals to man "truth in the wider, *pragmatic* sense of the word," one doesn't, remembering Aztec human sacrifices or the self-immolation of Indian widows, know whether to laugh or cry.

The odd and instructive thing in all this, however— and my point in restating here these by now familiar arguments—is that Malinowski's defective conception of religion stemmed not so much from an insensitivity to spiritual concerns as such (he had, in fact, a keener appreciation of the urgency of such concerns than is common among anthropologists) as from a defective conception of precisely that aspect of culture whose centrality he was so determined to establish: the everyday life of man in the world.

Malinowski was not wrong in his instinct that the ordinary world of commonsense objects and practical acts, of conventional wisdom and received prejudices, of things everybody knows, judgments everybody makes, feelings everybody has, is, to borrow a phrase from Alfred Schutz, the paramount reality in human experience—paramount in the sense that it is the world in which we are most solidly rooted, whose inherent actuality we can hardly question, and from whose pressures and requirements we can at best but temporarily escape. Where he was wrong was in seeing this world as consisting of techniques for coping with life rather than as consisting of a way, one way, of conceiving of it. For, at base, common sense is not folk technology; it is not even folk knowledge: it is a frame of mind. Rather than "a crude empiry . . . a body of practical and technical abilities, rules of thumb and of art having no theoretical value," as Malinowski called it, common sense consists of a body of assumptions, some of them conscious but the bulk merely taken for granted, about the way things in the simple nature of the case are—about what is normal and what is not, what is reasonable and what is not, what is real and what is not.

From this point of view, an understanding of what, as a way of looking at life (that is to say, of living it) common sense is, is indeed prior to the understanding of religion as such a way, a different way, of looking at it. This is not because religion is a disguised extension of common sense, as Malinowski would have it, but because, like art, science, ideology, law, or history, it springs from a perception of the insufficiency of commonsense notions to the very task to which they are dedicated: making sense out of experience. The everyday world of what everyone who has eyes to see sees and ears to hear hears may indeed be paramount: a man (or even large groups of men) can be aesthetically insensitive, religiously unconcerned, unequipped to pursue scientific analysis, and ignorant of history; but he cannot be completely lacking in common sense and survive. But, for most people anyway, this sort of matter-of-fact realism is hardly, as we say, enough; it leaves, as we also say, something to be desired.

It is true that many individuals in all societies never get much closer to an historical frame of mind than "let the dead bury the dead," to a scientific one than "feed a cold and starve a fever," to an aesthetic one than "I know what I like," to a religious one than "God takes care of children, drunks, and the United States of America." But it is equally true that for some people in every society (and, though I cannot really prove it, probably for every unretarded adult in some aspect of his life) this sort of flat-footed "everything is what it is and not another thing" approach to experience just won't do. For some people the fact that the good die young and the evil flourish as the green bay tree gets to them. For others the drama of a sea storm or the grace of a running deer does. For others some sort of what-came-before-the-beginning or what-will-happen-after-the-end sort of problem absorbs them. That votary of the commonsense persuasion, Samuel Butler, to the contrary notwithstanding, to know what's what is *not* as high as any metaphysic can fly.

What this means in terms of the analysis of culture is that we must view art, history, philosophy, science, or, in the case at hand, religion, against the background of commonsense notions to see how they grow out of them, go beyond them and, so it is claimed anyway, complete and deepen them. Not only is there a movement to break through the incrustation of common sense, but there is a return to the world of the obvious and ordinary, to correct and change it in light of what has been learned, or thought to have been learned, by transcending it. Our image of the facts of life is less artless than it looks; it is fashioned and re-fashioned in terms of specialized cultural enterprises which grow out of and away from it and then react, like so many second thoughts, back upon it. There is a dialectic between religion and common sense—as there is between art, science, and so on and common sense—which necessitates their being seen in terms of one another. Religion must be viewed against the background of the insufficiency, or anyway the felt insufficiency, of common sense as a total orientation toward life; and it must also be viewed in terms of its formative impact upon common sense, the way in which, by questioning the unquestionable, it shapes our apprehension of the quotidian world of "what there is" in which, whatever different drummers we may or may not hear, we are all obliged to live.

There has been, in short, a general shift in modern anthopological discussion of culture, and within it of religion as a part of culture, a shift from a concern with thought as an inner mental state or stream of such states to a concern with thought as the utilization by individuals in society of public, historically created vehicles of reasoning, perception, feeling, and understanding—symbols, in the broadest sense of the term. In the study of religion, this shift is in the process of altering our entire view of religious experience and its social and psychological impact. The focus is now neither on subjective life as such nor on outward behavior as such, but on the socially available "systems of significance"— beliefs, rites, meaningful objects—in terms of which subjective life is ordered and outward behavior guided.

Such an approach is neither introspectionist nor behaviorist; it is semantic. It is concerned with the collectively created patterns of meaning the individual uses to give form to experience and point to action, with conceptions embodied in symbols and clusters of symbols, and with the directive force of such conceptions in public and private life. So far as religion is concerned, the problem becomes one of a particular sort of perspective, a particular manner of interpreting experience, a certain way of going at the world as opposed to other ways, and the implications such a perspective has for conduct. The aim of the comparative study of religion is (or anyway, ought to be) the scientific characterization of this perspective: the description of the wide variety of forms in which it appears; the uncovering of the forces which bring these forms into existence, alter them, or destroy them; and the assessment of their influences, also various, upon the behavior of men in everyday life.

But how are we to isolate the religious perspective at all? Are we not thrown back once more upon the necessity of defining "religion," adding one more catch phrase—"the belief in spiritual beings," "morality touched with emotion," "ultimate concern"— to what is surely an endless catalog? Must we not go yet once more through the familiar exercise of sorting out "religion" from "superstition," "religion" from "magic," "religion" from "philosophy," "religion" from "custom," from "folklore," from "myth," from "ceremony"? Does not all understanding, or anyway all scientific understanding, depend upon an initial isolation, a laboratory preparation, so to speak, of what it is that one is trying to understand?

Well, no. One can begin in a fog and try to clear it. One can begin, as I have in this book, with an assortment of phenomena almost everyone but the professionally contrary will regard as having something vaguely to do with "religion" and seek for what it is that leads us to think so, what it is that leads us to think that these rather singular things certain people do, believe, feel, or say somehow belong together with sufficient intimacy to submit to a common name. This is, I admit, a definitional procedure also, but a definitional procedure of a more inductive sort, rather more comparable to noting the oblique resemblances in the way in which Dubliners talk or Parisians walk than to filtering out pure substances. We look not for a universal property—"sacredness" or "belief in the supernatural," for example—that divides religious phenomena off from nonreligious ones with Cartesian sharpness, but for a system of concepts that can sum up a set of inexact similarities, which are yet genuine similarities, we sense to inhere in a given body of material. We are attempting to articulate a way of looking at the world, not to describe an unusual object.

The heart of this way of looking at the world, that is, of the religious perspective, is, so I would like to argue, not the theory that beyond the visible world there lies an invisible one (though most religious men have indeed held, with differing degrees of sophistication, to some such theory); not the doctrine that a divine presence broods over the world (though, in an extraordinary variety of forms, from animism to monotheism, that too has been a rather popular idea); not even the more diffident opinion that there are things in heaven and earth undreamt of in our philosophies. Rather, it is the conviction that the values one holds are grounded in the inherent structure of reality, that between the way one ought to live and the way things really are there is an unbreakable inner connection. What sacred symbols do for those to whom they are sacred is to formulate an image of the world's construction and a program for human conduct that are mere reflexes of one another.

In anthropology, it has become customary to refer to the collection of notions a people has of how reality is at base put together as their world view. Their general style of life, the way they do things and like to see things done, we usually call their ethos. It is the office of religious symbols, then, to link these in such a way that they mutually confirm one another. Such symbols render the world view believable and the ethos justifiable, and they do it by invoking each in support of the other. The world view is believable because the ethos, which grows out of it, is felt to be authoritative; the ethos is justifiable because the world view, upon which it rests, is held to be true. Seen from outside the religious perspective, this sort of hanging a picture from a nail driven into its frame appears as a kind of sleight of hand. Seen from inside, it appears as a simple fact.

Religious patterns such as those I have been discussing thus have a double aspect: they are frames of perception, symbolic screens through which experience is interpreted; and they are guides for action, blueprints for conduct. Indonesian illumination-ism portrays reality as an aesthetic hierarchy culminating in a void, and it projects a style of life celebrating mental poise. Moroccan maraboutism portrays reality as a field of spiritual ener-gies nucleating in the persons of individual men, and it projects a style of life celebrating moral passion. Kalidjaga in classical Morocco would not be heroic but unmanly; Lyusi in classical Java would not be a saint but a boor.

The world view side of the religious perspective centers, then, around the problem of belief, the ethos side around the problem of action. As I say, these are, within the confines of faith, not only inseparable, they are reflexes of one another. Yet for analytical purposes, I want to separate them here momentarily and, using the Moroccan and Indonesian cases as reference points, discuss them independently. Having done that, the general relevance of these particular cases for the understanding of religion as such should be more readily apparent, as should the usefulness (I would claim no more for it than that) of this whole approach to the comparative study of it.

The major characteristic of religious beliefs as opposed to other sorts of beliefs, ideological, philosophical, scientific, or common-sensical, is that they are regarded as being not conclusions from experience—from deepened social awareness, from reflective spec-ulation and logical analysis, from empirical observation and hy-pothesis testing, or from matriculation in the school of hard knocks—but as being prior to it. For those who hold them, reli-gious beliefs are not inductive, they are paradigmatic; the world, to paraphrase a formulation of Alisdair MacIntyre's, provides not evidences for their truth but illustrations of it. They are a light cast upon human life from somewhere outside it.

Social scientists, including anthropologists, have generally not been comfortable with this way of formulating things, not only because most of them are nonbelievers (as, indeed, I myself am), but because it seems to involve a departure from the path of strict empiricism. But there is nothing unempirical (though there is a great deal that is difficult) about describing the way in which religious belief appears to the believer. In fact, not to do so is to shrink from carrying empiricism into realms where, for reasons which perhaps demand a psychoanalytical explanation more than a methodological one, the researcher feels lost and threatened. It is also, and this is more important, to neglect to ask (or even to recognize) some of the most critical scientific questions in this whole field of study, not the least of which is, "How is it that believers are able to believe?" Or, to risk even more being taken for an apologist for something otherworldly, "Whence comes faith?"

Theological answers aside, it is clear that it comes from the social and psychological workings of religious symbols. To use "religious" here may seem an egregious begging of the question, but only if one conceives of each person coming into a culture-less world and then spinning such a world around him out of the substance of his inner self, as a spider spins his web out of his abdomen. This is, of course, not the case: for any given individual certain acts, objects, tales, customs, and so on are already considered by the members of his society, or anyway some of them, to mediate a valid world view by the time he is born into it. Kalidjaga found the illuminationist tradition of Madjapahit waiting for him when he decided to turn from thievery to self-sanctification; Lyusi had the maraboutic tradition of the Berber dynasties waiting for him when he descended from the Atlas to become a reformer of sultans. Sukarno and Muhammed V were born into even more opulent cultural circumstances. Just as no man has to invent a language in order to speak, so no man has to invent a religion in order to worship; though it is true that he has rather more of an option (particularly, but not exclusively, in modern societies) as to whether he will worship than as to whether he will speak. Commonsense skills are, again, by and large obligatory for anyone who is to thrive at all, where spiritual ones are not. You don't have to have a soul, as Don Marquis once said, unless you really want one.

The main context, though not the only one, in which religious symbols work to create and sustain belief is, of course, ritual. It is the prayers and festivals around a saint's tomb, the exaltation and bead-telling in a brotherhood lodge, and the obsessive submissiveness surrounding the Sultanate that keep maraboutism going; private meditation, etherialized art, and state ceremonialism that nourish illuminationism. Individuals can, and in Indonesia and Morocco a few do, attain a concept of cosmic order outside of these institutions specifically dedicated to inculcating such a concept (though even in such cases there must be support from cultural symbols in some form or other). For the overwhelming majority of the religious in any population, however, engagement in some form of ritualized traffic with sacred symbols is the major mechanism by means of which they come not only to encounter a world view but actually to adopt it, to internalize it as part of their personality.

The reasons why particular individuals are susceptible to the workings of sacred symbols at all, why they engage in rituals and why the rituals have (or, conversely, fail to have) an effect, is of course another problem. Part of the answer is surely psychological, having to do with individual needs for nurturance, for external authority, or whatever, as well as capacities for trust, affection, and so on. Part, too, is surely social. In nonindustrial societies particularly, the social pressures toward religious conformity are very great, and they are not so weak in all parts of industrial society as is sometimes represented. In Morocco and Indonesia such pressures remain very strong, and though in some cases they lead to mere superficial conformity, in most they lead, so I would judge from my observations, to a significant degree of genuine faith. The notion that the demand for religious conformity can produce hypocrites but not believers is simply wrong. It is difficult to say whether more men have achieved faith because it was expected of them than have achieved it because they were internally driven toward it; and perhaps, as both factors are always involved to some degree, the question is pointless. But it would not do to adopt too much of an inner-compulsion view on the matter.

In any case, besides the psychological and sociological factors impelling men toward belief, there are also cultural ones, arising, as I suggested, from the felt inadequacies of commonsense ideas in the face of the complexities of experience. It was this recognition that life continually overflows the categories of practical reason that Max Weber called "the problem of meaning," and it is most familiar to us, given the intense ethicism of the West, in the form of the problem of evil: "Why do the just suffer and the unjust prosper?" But it has many more dimensions, for the events through which we live are forever outrunning the power of our ordinary, everyday moral, emotional, and intellectual concepts to construe them, leaving us, as a Javanese image has it, like a water buffalo listening to an orchestra. And one way, at least, to attempt to deepen these concepts is to supplement them with the revelations of a wider order provided by religion. Whatever else "Islam"—maraboutic, illuminationist, or scripturalist—does for those who are able to adopt it, it surely renders life less outrageous to plain reason and less contrary to common sense. It renders the strange familiar, the paradoxical logical, the anomalous, given the recognized, if eccentric, ways of Allah, natural.

In societies like those of classical Morocco and Indonesia, then, psychological, social, and cultural factors converge to move men toward participation in the established religious rituals and toward the acceptance of the metaphysical beliefs implicit in such rituals. In such societies, believing is, so to speak, easy, almost as easy as speaking. This is, however, not to say that it is universal, as is sometimes claimed. There is a great deal of skepticism, usually only partial skepticism, but skepticism nonetheless, in traditional societies. The inevitable tension which remains between the deliverances of common sense and even the most compelling and comprehensive religion assures that, as does the widespread employment of religiously based power to less than elevated ends.

"Beware a woman from the front," a Moroccan maxim runs, "a mule from behind, and a marabout from all directions." And in Indic Java, that enchanted garden presided over by royal gods, the peasants used to say, "At night everything we have belongs to the thieves; in the daytime everything we have belongs to the king." But in general, men accepted the reality of maraboutism, whatever they may have thought of the claims of the character of individual marabouts, the divinity of kingship, whatever they may have thought about how actual kings behaved. Psychologically, socially, and culturally, it was the natural, the commonsensical thing to do. Even today, men who are unbelievers in the total sense, and there are very few of them, still tend to be regarded, both in Morocco and Java, less as wicked than as mad.

It is this religious ease that the changes of the last century and a half, not only in Morocco and Indonesia, but in the world generally, have progressively undermined. Inner need, community pressure, and the problems of meaning no longer converge so powerfully to impel the individual toward ritualized contact with sacred symbols. The symbols are still there, of course; so, for the most part, are the rituals, and they are still generally regarded as housing imperishable spiritual truths. But now people find it harder and harder, so to speak, to make them work, more and more difficult to draw out of them the settled sense of moving with the deepest grain of reality that defines the religious mind.

As I have said several times, this process is only slightly advanced in Morocco and Indonesia, though it is rapidly gaining momentum. In the United States, where church attendance reaches new highs while the ability to internalize the Christian world view continues, apparently, to decline, it has gone much further. Whether the process, here, or elsewhere, is reversible, which I rather doubt, or whether, even in the interests of religion, it ought to be reversed, which I doubt even more, is, for the moment, beside the point. The fact is that the loss of power of classical religious symbols to sustain a properly religious faith, which the recent history of both Morocco and Indonesia displays, is general. So too, I think, is the major reason for this loss—the secularization of thought; so too, the major response to it—the ideologization of religion.

The secularization of thought in the modern world has had many causes and taken many forms; but on the cultural level it is in great part a result of the explosive growth of another trans-commonsensical cultural perspective, which is at the same time its main embodiment: positive science. In its pure form, the diffusion of the scientific way of looking at things to Third World countries like Morocco and Indonesia has been relatively slight. But the awareness that everyday experiences can be set in a broader and more meaningful context by resort to symbols which picture reality in terms of general laws inductively established as well as by resort to those which picture it in terms of fixed paradigms authoritatively revealed has spread to virtually every corner of either society. Even a century ago religious beliefs were about the only means available for plugging leaks in the hand-crafted dike of common sense. Today even the humblest peasant or shepherd knows that that is no longer so.

The long, rather unedifying history of the warfare between science and religion in the West has tended to lead in this century to the comfortable conclusion that "at base" they are not really in conflict. In the sense that one cannot subject expressions of faith to scientific tests nor disprove natural laws by quoting scripture, this is no doubt true. It is also no doubt true that there is no inherent reason why the view of reality generated by traffic with scientific symbols, in laboratories or wherever, need contradict the view of it generated by traffic with religious symbols, in mosques or wherever. And clearly, science and religion are not responses to exactly the same sort of inadequacies of common sense. Their fields of concern, though they overlap, are far from coincident, and they are not, therefore, simple alternatives.

But for all this, the brute empirical fact is that the growth of science has made almost all religious beliefs harder to maintain and a great many virtually impossible to maintain. Even if they are not direct antitheses, there is a natural tension between the scientific and religious ways of attempting to render the world

comprehensible, a tension which need not, in my opinion probably will not, perhaps even cannot, eventuate in the destruction
of either of them, but which is nonetheless real, chronic, and increasingly intense. Unless the importance of this "struggle for
the real" is recognized and not passed off with easy pieties on either side, the history of religion, Islam or any other, in our times
is, scientifically anyway, unintelligible. The warfare between
science and religion (it is really rather more a succession of ran-
dom skirmishes, brief, confused, and indecisive, than a real war)
is not only not over; it is quite likely never going to end.

The scripturalists were at once the group in either society who
felt this tension between the progressive secularization of thought
in the modern world and the essentials of the religious perspective most keenly and who made the most vigorous response to it.
The turn toward an exclusivist emphasis on the written sources
of Islamic faith at the expense of those of the sort represented by
Moroccan saint worship or Indonesian self-communion, a turn
which was itself in part stimulated by the florescence of the scientific perspective in the West, made that tension, if not greater,
surely less evadable. Again, the confrontation with the scientific
way of looking at things was made directly only by the most advanced leaders of the movement, and even there the internaliza-
tion of that way of looking at things was very partial at best. But
the simple fact that for the scripturalists Islam became a set of
explicit dogmas to defend projected them into the middle of the
struggle for the real long before the more traditionalist groups
in either society were even aware that it was going on.

Scripturalism was, in fact, the main agency in both societies,
of what I have called, perhaps not altogether satisfactorily, the
ideologization of religion, and it is on these grounds rather than
its theological contributions, which were minor, that its adherents deserve to be called innovators. What the scripturalist movement accomplished, and having accomplished it, moved away
from the center of the stage in favor of nationalism and the religious neo-traditionalism which accompanied it, was to provide
a general policy for Islam vis-à-vis the modern world, a public

stance for it to take in a cultural setting in which secular modes of understanding (not only science, which I have here made stand for the whole complex, but modern philosophy, historiography, ethics, even aesthetics as well) play the axial role that in classical societies was played by religious ones. Scripturalism began, in our countries anyway, but I suspect, suitably redefined for other cultures or other faiths, elsewhere as well, the intellectual revolution of which the more explicitly political concepts which accompanied and followed independence were the culmination. The scripturalists taught not just their followers but even more importantly their opponents how to formulate the ideals of an established civilization in such a way that they could survive, for a while anyway, in a modern world more than a little inhospitable to them.

There were essentially two strategies, not merely in our countries but in the movement generally, which the scripturalists devised for pursuing the struggle for the real: the absolute separation of religious matters from scientific ones, and the attempt to show that the scriptures, especially the Koran, anticipate and are fully consonant with the spirit and findings of modern science. The first approach consists of a denial of any metaphysical significance whatsoever to science, in fact to secular reason in any form at all; its competence is strictly confined to the understanding of nature considered as some kind of mundane, self-contained system. Faith and reason are simply quarantined from one another, lest the former be contaminated and the latter shackled. The second approach consists of interpreting science as but an explicit spelling out of what is already implicitly present in religion, an extension and specification of the religious perspective rather than an autonomous mode of thought.

Taken together, these two notions make up a kind of Islamic deism: doctrinal essentials are protected from any sort of challenge by being locked away from human experience, while secular reason is left free to operate with full sovereignty in the ordinary world with the certain confidence that its findings can raise no problems for religious belief because such belief already implies them. "To reflect on the essence of the Creator [that is to say, on matters of religious belief in general]," Abduh wrote "is forbidden to the human intellect because of the severance of all relations between the two existences." On the other hand, however, "the summons of Islam to reflection in regard to created things is not in any way limited or conditioned, because of the knowledge that every sound speculation leads to a belief in God as He is described in the Koran." Or as Kenneth Cragg has more succinctly put it: "Dogmas held to be inviolate co-exist with freedoms commended as entire."

As by now might be expected, these two sides of the scripturalist response to the challenge posed by the secularization of thought have been differentially represented in our two societies. Both are present in both. But Indonesia, with her ingrained inclination to try to absorb all styles of thought into one broad, syncretic stream, has been naturally more receptive to the argument that Islamic doctrine and scientific discovery are really not conflicting but complementary forms of belief; while Morocco, with her as deeply ingrained inclination toward religious prefectionism and moral rigor, has been more receptive to the attempt to isolate a purified Islamic faith from contamination with everyday life. Scripturalism in both countries was and is a counter-tradition, against illuminationism and against maraboutism. But its adherents are still Indonesians and Moroccans, and they have not been able to escape, even in their reformism, what I have called the Fabianism of the one civilization and the Utopianism of the other. The Indonesian scripturalists have sought, like the kijaji I quoted in the previous chapter, to portray science, and indeed secular thought in general, as but an expression of Islam, merely another, for practical purposes perhaps more useful, way of putting what with greater depth if not equal explicitness the Koran has already said. Moroccan scripturalists have sought, contrariwise, to purge religious life of what they regarded as superstition in order both to restore an idealized, hermetic Islam and to liberate secular life from doctrinal constraints. In the one case, science poses no threat to faith because it is seen as religious; in the other, it poses no threat because it is seen as not.

With the sort of irony which often attends reformist movements, the achievements of scripturalism in providing an ideological stance for Islam in the modern world were applied with even more effectiveness in the service of the classical religious styles against which its reforms were primarily directed. As nationalism grew out of scripturalism, it also grew away from it and turned for its spiritual roots back toward the more established patterns of belief of the two countries. But in reconciling the world views projected by these patterns to the modern world it adopted the strategies that scripturalism had already developed for similar purposes. Indeed, it carried the process of the ideologization of religion, the movement from religiousness toward religious-mindedness, to its final stages. Sukarno's revival of the theater state in the guise of revolutionary nationalism and Muhammad V's revival of maraboutism in the same guise rested on the production of a kind of all-embracing secular religiosity in the first case and on a radical disjunction between personal piety and public life in the second. Whether these revamped traditions, having been constructed, can now persist depends upon whether the pattern of life they imply is viable in a semi-modern nation-state in the latter part of the twentieth century.

But this brings us to the guides-for-action side of religious symbols—to their influence upon how men actually behave.

In turning to the way in which religious belief exercises its effect on ordinary behavior, insofar as it actually exercises such an effect, there arises a peculiar problem that I would like to approach in what might seem a peculiar way. The religious perspective, like the scientific, the aesthetic, the historical, and so on, is after all adopted by men only sporadically, intermittently. Most of the time men, even priests and anchorites, live in the everyday world and see experience in practical, down-to-earth terms—they must, if they are to survive. Further, the main setting in which the religious perspective, in the proper sense of the term, is adopted is, as I have said, in ritual, or at least in some special sort of socio-psychological context different from the ordinary run of life, some distinctive sort of activity or some particular kind of mood. It is then that baraka is sensed rather than merely discussed, the void penetrated rather than merely theorized about, the Koranic message heard rather than merely applauded. Even the pious to see life in transtemporal terms only at moments.

There are a number of implications of this fact. The first is methodological and may be mentioned here more as a way into the other, more substantive implications than for its own sake, though it is not without relevance to the general arguments I have been making. Because religious perception, the actual employment of sacred symbols to activate faith, takes place in special settings and in particular rituals, it is clear that it is extremely difficult to get phenomenologically accurate descriptions of religious experience. When anthropologists (or anyone else who takes an empirical approach to the subject) talk to people about their religion—which, of course, no matter how much sheer observation we carry out or how many theological treatises we read, we must do if we are to understand anything at all—it is almost invariably in a setting about as far removed from the properly religious as it is possible to get. We talk to them in their homes, or the morning after some ceremony, or at best while they are passively watching a ritual. Rarely, if ever, can we get at them when they are really involved in worship.

There is, in fact, a contradiction in the mere supposition of doing so: for talking to an anthropologist or sociologist or psychologist *about* one's religious experiences is quite incompatible with actually at the moment undergoing them. Worship and analysis are simply impossible to carry out together, for the one involves being thoroughly involved, caught up, absorbed in one's experience, in what one is living through, while the other involves standing back and, with a certain detachment, looking at it.

I suppose that once this point is stated it seems so obvious as to be trivial. But it has gone virtually unrecognized, or at least undiscussed, in the comparative study of religion, and it has some rather more serious consequences for that study than might be imagined. The most important of these is that even with the best will in the world an informant will have some difficulty in recapturing and formulating what religion amounts to for him, and indeed he is almost certain to render it in terms of common-sense stereotypes and rationalizations which are useful for understanding common sense but may be positively misleading if taken for veridical reports of what goes on in a ritual, the recital or hearing of a myth, the curing of a patient, or whatever.

One way, perhaps, to make clearer what I am driving at and what this apparent digression has to do with the question of belief and action is by recourse to Freud's work on dreams, in particular to his concept of the "secondary revision" involved in the reporting of them. In fact, one of the greatest contributions, perhaps it is *the* greatest contribution, in *The Interpretation of Dreams* is Freud's full recognition and full facing up to just the methodological dilemma I am referring to here. The whole book is a monument to making a virtue out of a necessity—the necessity of having very indirect access to one's primary data. For the dreamer too is absorbed in his experience while dreaming, takes it, for all its wild irrationality, as profoundly real and can report on it only after he awakes. And then he will, as we all know, forget parts of it, most of it probably, and distort and elaborate the rest under the attempt to make it "make sense."

The situation in religious studies is hardly different. Sometimes, as with Indonesian trance experiences, the subject simply often remembers nothing at all afterward unless the vague sense, which is also a conviction, that he has had one hell of an experience can be counted as a memory. Other times, say after worshiping at a marabout's tomb, the subject may remember something but so cover it over with secondary revision that most of its vitality and real meaning, meaning for him, is lost or anyway uncommunicated. So far as we are concerned with religion as a perspective, with the meaningful interpretation it gives to experience, we necessarily see it through a pretty dark glass.

Of course, no more than dream interpretation is impossible is the analysis of religion, particularly if the secondary revision problem is recognized and, as with Freud, itself analyzed and dealt with. But that is an aside here. What is not an aside, and indeed is the key to the question of how religion shapes social behavior, is that much of religion's practical effect, like much of dreaming's, comes in terms of a kind of pale, remembered reflection of religious experience proper, in the midst of everyday life. Men, or anyway religious men, move back and forth between the religious perspective and the commonsense one with great frequency, the greater the more religious they are, and, like a repetitive dream, a repetitive religious experience—an amnesic trance or an imperative offering—comes in time to haunt daily life and cast a kind of indirect light upon it. Some of the most important social effects of religion (though not, of course, the only ones) come through this oblique sort of what I called earlier reconstruction of common sense. Proximate, everyday acts come to be seen, if vaguely and indistinctly, subliminally almost, in ultimate contexts, and the whole quality of life, its ethos, is subtly altered. A clear distinction between religion experienced and religion remembered is thus an important analytical tool for understanding some otherwise difficult to understand phenomena. And not the least of these is the problem of the relation between belief and action.

When men turn to everyday living they see things in everyday terms. If they are religious men, those everyday terms will in some way be influenced by their religious convictions, for it is in the nature of faith, even the most unwordly and least ethical, to claim effective sovereignty over human behavior. The internal fusion of world view and ethos is, or so I am arguing, the heart of the religious perspective, and the job of sacred symbols is to bring about that fusion. Yet the revelatory encounter with such symbols does not take place in the everyday, commonsensical world, but in social contexts which are, necessarily, somewhat detached from it. What religious men have to work with in everyday life is not the immediate perception of the really real, or what they take to be such, but the memory of such a perception. Like the philosophers in Plato's cave, they are back in a world of shadows they interpret in a different way as a result of having been, for a moment, in the sunlight. But unlike the philosophers in Plato's cave, their problem, in this connection anyway, is not so much to communicate what things look like outside the cave as to make something more meaningful out of what goes on within it.

Or, to put aside images (which is very difficult to do when speaking of such matters), religious belief has its effect on common sense not by displacing it but by becoming part of it. Kalidjaga meditating is one thing; Kalidjaga, having meditated, setting out to found Mataram is another. Lyusi praying in the graveyard is one thing; Lyusi, having prayed, humbling Mulay Ismail is another. Religious belief in the midst of ritual, where it engulfs the total person, connecting him, as far as he is concerned, to the deepest foundations of existence, and religious belief as the amalgam of ideas, precepts, judgments, and emotions that the experience of that engulfment insinuates into the temper of everyday life are simply not the same thing. The former is the source of the latter; but it is the latter which shapes social action.

How far it shapes it, and in what ways, is, of course, another problem. And here it is necessary to make a distinction between what I would call the *force* of a cultural pattern (not just religion, but any symbol system men use to construe experience) and what I would call its *scope*.

By "force" I mean the thoroughness with which such a pattern is internalized in the personalities of the individuals who adopt it, its centrality or marginality in their lives. We all know that such force differs between individuals. For one man, his religious commitments are the axis of his whole existence, his faith is what he lives for and would quite willingly die for; he is god-intoxicated, and the demands flowing into everyday life from religious belief take clear precedence over those flowing into it from any other source—scientific knowledge, aesthetic experience, moral concern, or even practical considerations. For another man, not necessarily less honestly believing, his faith is worn more lightly, engages his personality less totalistically; more worldly, he subordinates other forms of understanding to religious ones less automatically and less completely. Then, too, other perspectives may dominate—there are scientific and aesthetic zealots as well as religious ones. And so on: the variations in such matters, even within single societies, is enormous. Speaking in statistical terms, however, in terms of averages and distributions, these differences also appear between whole populations. It is difficult to prove, but no one who has spent much time with Indonesians and Moroccans is likely to doubt that, on the whole, the latter take their religion a good deal more determinedly (which again is not to say necessarily more genuinely) than the former. Look, in this connection, at the Indians and the Chinese, the Irish and the French, the Scots and the Prussians. Men equally believing may not be equally devout.

By "scope" on the other hand, I mean the range of social contexts within which religious considerations are regarded as having more or less direct relevance. Obviously, force and scope are related in that a man for whom religion is personally important will naturally be inclined to extend its dominion over very wide ranges of life—to discern the Hand of God in everything from stomach aches to election returns. Yet they are not the same thing. The force of religion is, generally speaking, greater in Morocco than in Indonesia, but, as I have suggested several times, its scope is narrower. In Indonesia, almost everything is tinged, if lightly, with metaphysical meaning, the whole of ordinary life has a faintly transcendental quality about it, and it is rather difficult to isolate one part of it in which religious beliefs and the attitudes derived from them play a more prominent role than any other. In Morocco, the bulk of ordinary life is secular enough to suit the most dedicated rationalist, and religious considerations, for all their intensity, are operative over only a few, fairly well demarcated regions of behavior, so that one gets a ruthlessness in, for example, commercial and political affairs which, at its most egregious, reminds one of the piquant combination of professional brutality and personal piety one finds in some American racketeers.

In any case, it is necessary, in discussing the way in which religious beliefs and the sentiments they engender are absorbed into the stream of daily life, to distinguish between a vertical dimension, so to speak, of the process and a horizontal one, between the psychological grip of a culture pattern and the social range of its application. If, for example, we ask the question, at the moment rather popular in intellectual circles, "Is there a revival of religion now going on in the United States?" we can see that much of the disagreement that ensues turns on judging what is to count as a "revival," an increase in force or an expansion in scope. Those who regard the revival as an illusion argue that the importance of religious beliefs, Catholic, Protestant, or Jewish, in the lives of individuals is not only weak but getting weaker. Those who think there is a genuine revival point to greater church membership and the increasing importance of religious organizations and religious professionals in critical social processes, such as those centering around civil rights or world peace.

The point, of course, is that they may both be right; that the force of religious conviction measured in terms of responsiveness to sacred symbols is no greater, that religious beliefs are of axial importance to only a shrinking handful of men, but at the same time the relevance of such beliefs, peripheral as they may be, to social concerns has recently been noticeably widened. The empirical point is not critical here. What is critical is that the complexities hidden in what seems to be a simple and straightforward question, how important is religious belief in the direction of human behavior, be recognized. Such recognition may or may not enable us to cope with the question; but it should at least put an end to facile answers.

In these terms we can, then, state somewhat more exactly what has happened and is happening, to "Islam" in our two countries. If the main impact of religious experience on human behavior comes through the dampened echoes of that experience in everyday life, then religious-mindedness is the attempt to sustain the echoes in the absence of the experience.

Over the centuries, and particularly in what I have called the classical period, roughly 1500 to 1800 in both countries, traffic with sacred symbols produced not only distinctive forms of faith but, parallel to those forms and congruent with them, also distinctive styles of life. World view and ethos reinforced one another because the way people thought they ought to live their lives and to a reasonable degree actually did live them and the truths they thought they apprehended at saintly tombs or shadow plays were in tune with one another, were locked together in an organic, indeed an immutable union. This is not to say that everyone was highly religious or that everyone behaved in some fixed and stereotyped manner. It is merely to say that the conceptions, values, and sentiments which guided everyday behavior were, in a powerful and significant way, influenced by what were taken to be, by those who had them, revelations of the basic order of existence. Spiritual responsiveness varied then as it varies now, probably just as widely. There was a gap between social ideals and social practice as there is now, probably just as broad. What is different now is that even the spiritually responsive find revelations hard to come by, while the lives of even the unresponsive continue in large part to be based upon the assumption that they are not.

The reflections, reverberations, projections—one searches for the right word here and none is really very good—of religious experience in daily life remain very important in both Morocco and Indonesia. But they are, increasingly, the reflections, reverberations, and projections of experiences had by others than those who now depend upon them for filling out the crude framework of common sense—spiritual afterimages, so to speak. Though naturally somewhat adjusted to changed conditions, the tone and temper of ordinary life is not all that different from what it was in classical times. By and large, the Indonesians are still, collectively and individually, as elusive as Kalidjaga; the

Moroccans still, collectively and individually, as emphatic as Lyusi. But for more and more of them the sort of ritually heightened consciousness of the really real (or supposed such) which gave rise to and justified this ethos and was in turn supported and made possible by it is inaccessible. I do not, again, want to overstress the degree to which this disjunction between the commonsensical and trans-commonsensical versions of belief, that is to say, religious-mindedness, has proceeded in our two countries. It has really just begun: in Morocco, barely; in Indonesia, a shadow more than barely. But it has begun and it is the way things are moving, have been moving for at least a century, and are, in my opinion, likely to keep on moving for some time. In other Third World states, say Tunisia or Egypt, to stick to Muslim examples, it has perhaps gone further. And in the West, it has gone very far indeed: we have a while to wait yet, I think, even in Tunisia or Egypt, before we see an explicit movement for a "religionless Islam" advancing under the banner, "Allah is dead."

In the meantime, we have the less undressed versions of religious-mindedness that I reviewed in the last chapter, scripturalism, the royalist neo-maraboutism of Muhammed V, and the syncretistic theatricalism of Sukarno. All are still in the field, all still seeking to render themselves credible as something more than passing isms. Each resorts to some spiritual afterimage—that of pristine Islam, that of the baraka-charged dynasty, or that of the exemplary state—to consolidate its position.

But so far, none has been able definitively to do so. For scripturalism to become a living religious tradition rather than merely a collection of strained apologies, its adherents would have to undertake a serious theological rethinking of the scholastic tradition they can, apparently, neither live with nor live without. But since Abduh, who, for all his hesitations and incoherencies, made a valiant attempt at such theological rethinking, virtually nothing has been done; certainly not in Indonesia and Morocco, where, a few marginal and not very impressive exceptions aside, critical reexamination of Islamic doctrine has never been even begun. The revival of the maraboutic Imamist tradition under

Muhammad V has not been carried forward into the new definition of the relation between spiritual values and mundane power
it seemed for a moment to promise, a definition which might
have, if not removed, at least eased the tension between holy man
and strong man which, at every level from sultan to local sheikh,
and often enough within the life of a single individual, continues
to plague Moroccan society. And as for Sukarno's hectic myth-
building and creed-mongering, which (though he never got
around to revising the calendar) reminds one of nothing so much
as the experiments in civil religion of the French Revolution, it
has simply failed to accomplish what, so self-consciously, it was
intended to accomplish: provide an eclectic, all-embracing national faith to which the spiritually divided Indonesian masses
could effectively repair.

So amid great changes, great dilemmas persist, as do the established responses to them. In fact the responses seem to grow
more pronounced as they work less well. The Moroccan disjunction between the forms of religious life and the substance of everyday life advances almost to the point of spiritual schizo-
phrenia. The Indonesian absorption of all aspects of life—religious, philosophical, political, scientific, commonsensical, even
economic—into a cloud of allusive symbols and vacuous abstractions is rather less prominent than it was two years ago; but its
progress has hardly been halted, much less reversed.

When I think of the religious situation in the two countries
today, and particularly of the relation between belief and action,
two images of young men come to mind, my last human metaphors to set beside Lyusi and Muhammed V, Kalidjaga and Sukarno. The first is a Moroccan student, a highly educated, French-
speaking, but traditionally raised *evolué*, as the sour vernacular
of French colonialism would call him, on an airplane bound for
New York, his first trip away from home, where he will study

at an American university. Frightened, as well he might be, by the experience of flying (as well as the thought of what awaits him when he lands), he passes the entire trip with the Koran gripped in one hand and a glass of scotch in the other. The second image is that of a brilliant mathematics and physics student, studying for an advanced degree at the University of Indonesia— one of the country's few promising scientists, the sort of man who will build their bomb if they ever get one—who explains to me for four hours an extremely complicated, almost cabalistic scheme in which the truths of physics, mathematics, politics, art, and religion are indissolubly, and to my mind indiscriminately, fused. He spends, he says, all of his free time working on this scheme, which means very much to him, for one cannot find one's way through modern life without, as he puts it, a compass.

Indeed, one cannot; but of what materials is such a compass to be constructed? Vagrant imaginings of a harmonized world? Sacred texts transformed to fetishes? Are intellectual castle-building and moral double-bookkeeping any longer useful strategies in the struggle for the real? Or are they now but desperate holding actions?—or, more, disguised retreats? And, if this is so, what will happen to men like these students when this fact comes clear? When the fact that they can neither drown life in a formless oneness nor parcel it neatly into severed realms becomes too apparent to be covered over with cosmic fantasies and routine observances? Frank O'Connor once remarked that no Irishman is really interesting until he has begun to lose his faith. The revelatory shocks that awaited Lyusi and Kalidjaga and rendered them interesting await our anxious traveler and muddled physicist, too, and with them the unquiet societies whose embodiments they are.

Bibliographical Note

As my text is general and summary, an essay rather than a treatise, so, also, is my documentary apparatus. I have made no attempt to make my arguments look less controversial, speculative, or inferential than they are by appending to them an extensive list of arcane references but have instead prepared the following brief bibliographical note, which is intended to serve not so much to support my interpretations as to lead those to whom they seem intriguing and worth further examination to some of the books and articles where such examination might logically begin. I have, as a result, keyed these references to the text only loosely, first by chapter and second by block of pages, noting in passing the sources of direct quotations. Something is lost in solidity this way; but something is gained in candor.

Chapter 1

Pages 4–9

The standard history of Morocco is H. Terasse, *Histoire du Maroc des Origines à L'ètablissement du Protectorat Francais*, 2 vols. Casablanca, 1949–50, but it ought not to be. There is much useful information in Terasse and some original and valuable ideas, but there is also a pervasive colonial bias and a rather, to my mind, simplistic interpretation of the course of Moroccan history. In the English abridgment of this work (*History of Morocco*, Casablanca, 1952), its virtues are discarded and its faults concentrated. A much better work, though more as a factual compendium, a chronicle, than an historical analysis, is Ch.-A. Julien, *Histoire de L'Afrique du Nord*, 2 vols. Paris, 1961, which

takes as its object the whole of North Africa rather than merely
Morocco. The best book on the development of North African
Islam, and indeed one of the finest books ever written on the area,
is A. Bel, *La Religion Musulmane en Berbérie*, *1*, Paris, 1938.
Projected as the first of three volumes, the others of which, alas,
never appeared, it stands as a promise of what can be done in the
field of North African history by someone who combines the
requisite scholarship with the requisite vision. N. Barbour's *Morocco*, London, 1965 (see also his—edited—*A Survey of North
Africa* [London, New York, Toronto, 1962], pp. 75–200) is the
best popular introduction to Moroccan history, and for North Africa as a whole, the brief chapter in C. Gallagher, *The United
States and North Africa* (Cambridge, Mass., 1963), pp. 39–115,
is a brilliant tour de force.

Pages 9–13

The best general history of Indonesia in English is still B.
Vlekke, *Nusantara, A History of Indonesia*, The Hague and Bandung, 1959; the best in Dutch, H. J. De Graaf, *Geschiedenis van
Indonesie*, The Hague and Bandung, 1949; though neither of
these gets very far below the surface of things. Some of the essays,
especially the early ones, in F. W. Stapel, ed., *Geschiedenis van
Nederlandsche-Indie*, 5 vols. Amsterdam, 1938–40, are useful, but
the fact is that a really major history of Indonesia as a whole—
"from earliest times to the present day"—remains to be written,
which, considering the range of linguistic and scholarly skills it
would demand, is not exactly surprising. Of the by now rather
large number of general Southeast Asian histories, most of them
superficial, by far the best is D. G. E. Hall, *A History of Southeast Asia*, London, 1955.

For a brief review of the development of the anthropological
analysis of religion, see my article, "Religion: Anthropological
Study," in *International Encyclopedia of the Social Sciences*,
New York, 1968.

Chapter 2

Pages 25–29

Material on Kalidjaga can be found in Th. Pigeaud's great *Javaanse Volksvertoningen* (Batavia, 1938), pp. 387–89, 395–98; in D. A. Rinkes, *De Heiligen van Java*, Batavia, 1910–13; and in G. W. J. Drewes, "The Struggle Between Javanism and Islam as Illustrated by the Serat Dermagandul," in *Bijdragen tot Taal-, Land- en Volkenkunde*, 122 (1966), 309–65. The best general works on the developments in the archipelago from the fourteenth to the seventeenth centuries are B. Schrieke, *Indonesian Sociological Studies: Selected Writings* (tr.), 2 vols. The Hague and Bandung, 1955, 1957; J. C. van Leur, *Indonesian Trade and Society* (tr.), The Hague and Bandung, 1955; and M. A. P. Meilink-Roelofsz, *Asian Trade and European Influence*, The Hague, 1962. I have developed the interpretation, here radically condensed, of this period in *The Development of the Javanese Economy: A Sociocultural Approach*, Center for International Studies, Massachusetts Institute of Technology, 1956 (mimeo.).

Pages 29–35

Jacques Berque's superb *Al-Yousi, Problèmes de la Culture Marocaine au XVIIème Siècle*, Paris and The Hague, 1958, gives a full description and analysis of Lyusi's life and work, as well as an outline of the social and cultural setting in which he operated. There is also a brief biography of Lyusi (there called "el-Ioûsî") in E. Lévi-Provencal, *Les Historiens des Chorfa* (Paris, 1922), pp. 269–72. The quotation from Berque on p. 31 is from *Al-Yousi*, p. 135; the poem on p. 31 is given on p. 20 of the same work. On the "Maraboutic Crisis" more generally, see Terasse, *Histoire du Maroc*, 2, 160 ff., 214 ff., and Julien, *Histoire de L'Afrique du Nord*, 2, 219 ff.

Pages 35–43

The major history of the Indic period is, despite all the corrections it has since been found necessary to make of it, still N. J. Krom, *Hindoe-Javaansche Geschiedenis,* 2d ed. The Hague, 1931. (See also his piece in Stapel, *Geschiedenis van N.-I., 1,* 119–298.) A brief, simple, but sociologically more realistic summary on the period can be found in W. F. Stutterheim, *Het Hinduisme in den Archipel,* Groningen and Batavia, 1932. On divine kingship and "the exemplary center" (not there called that), see R. Heine-Geldern, "Conceptions of State and Kingship in Southeast Asia," *Far Eastern Quarterly,* 2 (1942), 15–30. On Indic-type state organization in general, see Pigeaud, *Java in the Fourteenth Century: A Study in Cultural History,* 5 vols. The Hague, 1960–63; G. Coedes, *Les Etats Hindouises d'Indochine et d'Indonesie,* Paris, 1948; G. P. Rouffaer, *Vorstenlanden,* Overdruk uit Adatrecht Bundel XXXIV, Serie P, No. 81 (Leiden, 1931), pp. 233–378; S. Moertono, "State and Statecraft in Old Java," unpublished Ph.D. dissertation, Ithaca, Cornell University, 1966; and my "Politics Past, Politics Present," *European Journal of Sociology,* 8 (1967), 1–14. On Indo-Javanese religio-political ideas, the numerous works of C. C. Berg should be consulted, but in a properly critical spirit. The two most general expressions of his point of view are probably his essay, "Javaansche Geschiedschriving," in Stapel, *Geschiedenis van N.-I.,* 2, 7–148, and "Javanese Historiography, A Synopsis of its Evolution," in Hall, ed., *Historians of South East Asia* (London, 1961), pp. 164–71. Some of the notions advanced in the text as elements of the Indic-Indonesian world view are discussed for contemporary Java in my *The Religion of Java* (Glencoe, Ill., 1960), esp. pp. 227–354.

The "copy of its capital" reference on p. 36 is in Pigeaud, *Java in the Fourteenth Century,* which, despite its title, is a translation of the *Negarakertagama* of 1365 A.D., accompanied by some contemporaneous texts together with notes, commentaries, a recapitulation, and a glossary. This reference is to canto 17, stanza

3; the Javanese text is in *1*, 14, the translation in *3*, 21. The sun reference which follows it in the text is in canto 12, stanza 6, with the Javanese in *1*, 10, the English in *3*, 15. The quotation, "The Retainer should honor his master" on p. 37 is from the *Rajapatingundala*, appended to the *Negarakertagama* translation in ibid., the Javanese in *1*, 10, the English (which I have altered slightly in the interests of clarity) in *3*, 135. Prapanca's remarks about the "helpless, bowed," quoted on p. 38, is from canto 1, stanza 5, of the *Negarakertagama*, the Javanese in *1*, 3, the English in *3*, 4.

On the "political division of labor" in colonial Indonesia, see J. S. Furnivall, *Netherlands India: A Study of a Plural Economy*, New York, 1944, and, by the same author, *Colonial Policy and Practice, A Comparative Study of Burma and Netherlands India*, Cambridge, 1948; A. Vandenbosch, *The Dutch East Indies, Its Government and Politics*, Berkeley and Los Angeles, 1942; and Schrieke, "The Native Rulers," in *Indonesian Sociological Studies*, 2, 169 ff. The "Byzantine" image is from Rouffaer and H. Juynboll, *Het Batik Kunst in Nederlandsche Indie en haar Geschiedenis*, The Hague, 1932.

Pages 43–54

On the rise of the Alawites, see Lévi-Provencal, *Les Historiens des Chorfa*. Bel's remark about sects and empires is in his *La Religion Musulmane en Berbérie*, p. 15; his *homme fétiches* phrase is introduced on p. 244; and his discussion of the Berber dynasties, though focused on their religious dimensions, is the most incisive I have seen. J. F. P. Hopkins, *Medieval Muslim Government in Barbary*, London, 1958, gives a clear and carefully researched picture of political organization at the time, and R. Le Tourneau, *Fez in the Age of the Merinides* (tr.), Norman, 1961, has some material on urban social life during this period. The Lévi-Provencal quotation on p. 47 is from *Les Historiens des Chorfa*, p. 10.

On saint worship, perhaps the best descriptive work is E. Dermenghem, *Le Culte des Saints dan L'Islam Maghrébin*, 6th ed.

Paris, 1956, but there is not much in the way of sociological analysis in it. E. Gellner's unfortuntely still unpublished Ph.D. dissertation, "The Role and Organization of a Berber Zawiya," University of London, 1957, is a fine study of a saint cult in action (the quotation on p. 51 about the saints *being* Islam is from this thesis). There is also much useful material compiled in E. A. Westermarck, *Ritual and Belief in Morocco*, 2 vols. London, 1926. Otherwise, discussions of saint worship in Morocco have tended to be either generalized or anecdotal.

As for brotherhoods, the most comprehensive work—again resolutely descriptive, almost to the point of mindlessness, but yet quite useful as a source—is G. Drague, *Equisse d'Histoire Religieuse du Maroc, Confréries et Zaouias*, Paris, n.d. (ca. 1951). (The figures on p. 51 are derived from this work, pp. 117–24, by making some assumptions about age and sex distributions in the 1939 population.) A briefer and more perceptive study is E. Michaux-Bellaire, *Essai sur L'Histoire des Confréries Marocaines*, Paris, 1921. There are, in addition, two excellent monographs on particular brotherhoods: R. Brunel, *Essai sur la Confrérie Religieuse des Aissaoua au Maroc*, Paris, 1926; and J. M. Abun-Nasr, *The Tijaniyya*, London, New York, Toronto, 1965. M. Lings' *A Moslem Saint of the Twentieth Century*, London, 1961, is a biography of an Algerian zawiya sheikh and has stimulated an interesting set of reflections on North African Sufism generally by Gellner, "Sanctity, Puritanism, Secularisation and Nationalism in North Africa. A Case Study," *Archives de Sociologie des Religions*, 15 (1963), 71–87. P. Marty, "Les Zaouias Marocaines et le Makhzen," *Revue des Etudes Islamiques* (1929), 575–600, gives the view from the *Residence* but is rather general.

The religious aspects of the Sultanate have not been discussed as thoroughly as they might, but there is some material in M. Lahbabi, *Le Gouvernement Marocain à L'Aube du XXe Siècle*, Rabat, 1958, and I. W. Zartman, *Destiny of a Dynasty*, Columbia, S.C., 1964. A full-scale investigation of the social and cultural bases of Alawite sovereignty remains, however, to be done.

The Berque phrase referred to on p. 52 is from his *Al-Youssi*, p. 135.

Chapter 3

Pages 62–65

The colonial period in both countries is, naturally enough, much more extensively documented than their histories generally but, also naturally enough, more subject to prejudiced and one-sided (both pro- and anti-imperialist) interpretations as well. Some of the more useful synoptic works, representing various points of view, include:

For Indonesia: Furnivall, *Netherlands India;* D. H. Burger, *De Ontsluiting van Java's Binnenland voor het Wereldverkeer,* Wageningen, 1939; Burger, "Structuurveranderingen in de Javaansche Samenleving," *Indonesie,* 2 (1948–49), 381–98, 521–37, and 3 (1949–50), 1–18, 101–23, 225–50, 347–50, 381–89, 512–34; W. F. Wertheim, *Indonesian Society in Transition,* 2d ed. The Hague and Bandung, 1959; Vandenbosch, *The Dutch East Indies;* A. D. E. de Kat Angelino, *Colonial Policy* (tr.), 2 vols. The Hague, 1931.

For Morocco: J-L. Miège, *Le Maroc et L'Europe,* 4 vols. (of five projected) Paris, 1961; Berque, *French North Africa, The Maghrib Between Two World Wars* (tr.), London, 1962; L. Cerych, *Européens et Marocains, 1930–1956,* Bruges, 1964; A. Maurois, *Lyautey,* Paris, 1931; E. Aubin, *Morocco of Today* (tr.), London, 1906.

Pages 65–70

There is no single synthetic work on the scripturalist movement in Indonesia—one must pick up one's data in small pieces from a variety of sources. I have tried to organize some of this material in some of my own work. See "Religious Belief and Economic Behavior in a Central Javanese Town: Some Preliminary Considerations," *Economic Development and Cultural Change,* 4 (1956) 134–58; "The Javanese Kijaji: The Changing

Role of Cultural Broker," *Comparative Studies in Society and History*, 2 (1960) 228–49; *The Religion of Java*, pp. 121–226; "Modernization in a Muslim Society: The Indonesian Case," in R. N. Bellah, ed., *Religion and Progress in Modern Asia* (New York, 1966), pp. 93–108; *Peddlers and Princes*, Chicago, 1963. For more primary material on some of the issues discussed in the text, see C. Snouck Hugronje, "De Hadjipolitiek der Indische Regeering," in his *Verspriede Geschriften* (Bonn and Leipzig, 1924), 4, pt. 2, 173–99; Hugronje, *Mekka in the Latter Part of the Nineteenth Century* (tr.), Leyden, 1931; Hugronje, "Brieven van een Wedono-pensioen, in *Verspriede Geschriften*, 4, pt. 1, 111–249; J. Vredenbregt, "The Hadj, Some of its Features and Functions in Indonesia," *Bijdragen tot Taal-, Land- en Volkenkunde*, 188 (1962), 91–154 (from which the figures concerning the hajj on p. 67 come); Pangeran Aria Achmad Djajadiningrat, *Herinneringen*, Amsterdan and Batavia, 1939.

With respect to the uprisings mentioned on pp. 68–69, see, for West Sumatra, M. Radjab, *Perang Paderi di Sumatera Barat* (*1803–1808*), Djakarta, 1954; for central Java, M. Yamin, *Sedjarah Peperangan Dipanegara, Pahlawan Kemerdekaan Indonesia*, Djakarta, 1952, and J. M. van der Kroef, "Prince Diponegoro: Progenitor of Indonesian Nationalism," *Far Eastern Quarterly*, 8 (1949), 429–50; for Northwest Java, S. Kartodirdjo, *The Peasants' Revolt of Banten in 1888, Its Conditions, Course and Sequel*, The Hague, n.d. (ca. 1966); on North Sumatra, Hugronje, *The Achehnese* (tr.), 2 vols. Leiden, 1906.

The rise of "reformism" is best detailed in H. Benda, *The Crescent and the Rising Sun* (The Hague and Bandung, 1958), pp. 9–99, and the entire book, despite its focus on the Japanese Occupation (i.e. 1942–45), is essential to anyone who wishes to understand "modern"—that is, "recent"—Islam in Indonesia. Wertheim, *Indonesia in Transition*, pp. 193–235, G.-H. Bousquet, *La Politique Musulmane et Coloniale des Pay-Bas*, Paris, 1939. and C. C. Berg, "Indonesia," in H. A. R. Gibb, ed., *Whither Islam? A Survey of Modern Movements in the Moslem World* (London, 1932), pp. 193 ff., also offer valuable discussions of reformism in Indonesia. Perhaps the simplest overall introduction to Islam in Indonesia is Bousquet, "Introduction a L'Étude de L'Islam Indonésien," *Revue des Études Islamiques*, 2–3 (1938), 133–259; though R. A. Kern, *De Islam in Indonesie*, The Hague, 1947, is also useful in this respect.

On the reform movement more generally, see K. Cragg, *Counsels in Contemporary Islam*, Edinburgh, 1965; W. Cantwell Smith, *Islam in Modern History*, Princeton, 1958; G. E. von Grunebaum, *Modern Islam, The Search for Cultural Identity*, Berkeley, 1926; Gibb, *Modern Trends in Islam*, Chicago, 1957; C. C. Adams, *Islam and Modernism in Egypt*, London, 1933.

Pages 70–74

The literature on Moroccan scripturalism is even less developed than on Indonesian, but useful material can be found in Allal Al-Fassi, *The Independence Movements of North Africa* (tr.), Washington, D.C., 1954; J. Abun-Nasr, "The Salafiyya Movement in Morocco: The Religious Basis of the Moroccan Nationalist Movement," in A. Hourani, ed., *St. Antony's Papers*, *16* (London, 1963), 90–105; D. Ashford, *Political Change in Morocco* (Princeton, 1961), pp. 29 ff.; Le Tourneau, "North Africa: Rigorism and Bewilderment," in von Grunebaum, ed., *Unity and Variety in Muslim Civilization*, Chicago, 1955; R. Rizette, *Les Partis Politiques Marocains* (Paris, 1955), pp. 6–27.

The "bismillah" anecdote comes from Lévi-Provencal, p. 20. The Al-Fassi quote on p. 72 is from Al-Fassi, *Independence Movements*, p. 112.

Concerning the pioneer religio-nationalist organizations, see, for Sarekat Islam: Benda, *The Crescent and the Rising Sun*, pp. 41 ff.; G. McT. Kahin, *Nationalism and Revolution in Indonesia* (Ithaca, 1952), pp. 65 ff.; R. van Niel, *The Emergence of the Modern Indonesian Elite* (The Hague and Bandung, 1960), pp. 101 ff.; R. Jay, *Religion and Politics in Rural Central Java* (New Haven, 1964), pp. 16 ff.

For Kutlat Al-'Amal Al-Watani: Al-Fassi, *Independence*

Movements; Rizette, *Les Partis Politiques Marocains,* pp. 68 ff.; Ashford, *Political Change,* pp. 35 ff.; Julien, *L'Afrique du Nord en Marche* (2d ed. Paris, 1952), pp. 146 ff.

Pages 74–82

On Muhammed V as such, see R. Landau, *Mohammed V,* Rabat, 1957; Landau, *Moroccan Drama* (San Francisco), pp. 199–205; R. Montagne, *Révolution au Maroc* (Paris, 1953), pp. 177–260; J. Lacouture, *Cinq Hommes et la France* (Paris, 1961). On the Sultanate as an institution, see Lahbabi, *Le Gouvernement Marocain;* Zartman, *Destiny of a Dynasty;* J. Robert, *La Monarchie Marocaine,* Paris, n.d. (ca. 1962); J. and S. Lacouture, *Le Maroc à L'Epreuve* (Paris, 1958). A number of earlier I-was-there type works give the flavor of the monarchy as it was at the end of the nineteenth or beginning of the twentieth century. Of these, among the best are Aubin, *Morocco of Today;* W. Harris, *Morocco That Was,* London, 1921; and F. Weisgerber, *Au Seuil du Maroc Moderne,* Rabat, 1947.

W. Montgomery Watt's theories concerning "autocratic" and "constitutional" concepts of legitimacy can be found in his *Islam and the Integration of Society,* London, 1961. See also his *Islamic Philosophy and Theology* (Edinburgh, 1962), pp. 53 ff.

The *blad l-makhzen/blad s-siba* contrast can be found at least mentioned in almost every recent book on Morocco and has now achieved the status of a stereotype—i.e. a concept more invoked than investigated. Perhaps the simplest presentation of it—where it is generalized to the whole of the Middle East—is in C. Coon, *Caravan, The Story of the Middle East* (New York, 1958), pp. 286–90, 309–23; but its greatest development is in the works of Robert Montagne, in whose hands it tends to turn into an ideological weapon. See, in this regard, his *Révolution au Maroc,* pp. 41–126, and *Les Berbères et le Makhzen dans le Sud du Maroc,* Paris, 1930.

On Moroccan nationalism generally, see Landau, *Moroccan Drama;* Ashford, *Political Change;* Gallagher, *The United States and North Africa,* pp. 84–115; Le Tourneau, *Evolution Poli-*

tique de L'Afrique du Nord Musulmane, 1920–1961 (Paris, 1962), pp. 223–51; Julien, *L'Afrique du Nord en Marche,* pp. 139–73, 339–95; Rizette, *Les Partis Politiques;* Al-Fassi, *Independence Movements;* Berque, *French North Africa.* The best discussion of the Berber Decree is in Berque, pp. 215–22; of the deposition, exile, and return of the Sultan, in Landau, pp. 295 ff. Gallagher places the Moroccan events most skillfully in the general North African setting (Julien's incisive work was, unfortunately, written before the various denouements, and so seems truncated). Al-Fassi best details the indigenous reaction, though as a *combattant* his view is, naturally enough, partial. Ashford's work is the most complete factually, but rather ill organized. A number of monographs specifically devoted to Moroccan nationalism, some by Moroccans, are apparently in process, so that in the next few years we should have a clearer picture of what is still, especially as compared to the Indonesian case, a not very well delineated movement.

The quotation from Julien on p. 80 is from *L'Afrique du Nord en Marche,* p. 146.

Pages 82–87

On Sukarno as such, see C. Adams, *Sukarno, an Autobiography,* Indianapolis, 1965; W. Hanna, *Bung Karno's Indonesia,* New York, 1961, pt. 2; L. Fisher, *The Story of Indonesia,* New York, 1959; "Soekarno, Dr. Ir.," *Ensiklopedia Indonesia* (Bandung and The Hague, n.d. [ca. 1956]), vol. M-N, p. 1265; N. Y. Nasution, *Ir. Sukarno, Riwajat Rinkas Penghidupan dan Perdjuangan,* Djakarta, n.d. (ca. 1951). On the Presidency as an institution, there is, aside from A. K. Pringgodigdo's brief and rather formalistic *The Office of President in Indonesia as Defined in Three Constitutions in Theory and Practice* (tr.), Ithaca, 1957, as yet no special study, but H. Feith, *The Decline of Constitutional Democracy in Indonesia,* Ithaca, 1962, provides much useful material and insight into its functioning, as does D. S. Lev, *The Transition to Guided Democracy,* Ithaca, 1966. On the reemergence of the classical style in the Sukarno Republik, see

A. R. Willner, *The Neo-Traditional Accommodation to Political Independence, The Case of Indonesia,* Princeton, 1966.

The "romanticism of revolution" quotation on p. 83 is given in Hanna, preface to *Bung Karno's Indonesia.*

Fieth's development of the contrast between "symbol manipulators" (or "solidarity makers") and "administrators" is to be found in his *Decline of Constitutional Democracy,* the outstanding work on postindependence politics in Indonesia. See also his "Indonesia's Political Symbols and their Wielders," *World Politics, 16* (1963), 79–97. On Indonesian nationalism, the sources are again numerous and of uneven quality and balance. Among the more useful are J. Th. P. Blumberger, *De Nationalistische Beweging in Nederlandsche-Indie,* Haarlem, 1931; J. M. Pluvier, *Overzicht van de Ontwikkeling der Nationalistsche Beweging in Indonesie in de Jaren 1930 tot 1942,* The Hague and Bandung, 1953; L. M. Sitorus, *Sedjarah Pergerakan Kebangsaan Indonesia,* Djakarta, 1947; Pringgodigdo, *Sedjarah Pergerakan Rakjat Indonesia,* Djakarta, 1950; D. M. G. Koch, *Om de Vrijheid,* Djakarta, 1950; and, most especially, Kahin, *Nationalism and Revolution.*

The development of "Marhaenism" has been outlined by Sukarno himself in a 1957 speech, "Marhaen and Proletarian" (tr.), Ithaca, 1960, of which my paragraphs on pp. 84–85 are a summary. Sukarno's early ideas and attitudes toward Islam —ideas and attitudes he never really seems to have altered—are most vividly presented in his *Surat Islam dari Endeh,* Bandung, 1931. On the Pantjasila, see his speech, "The Birth of the Pantjasila" (tr.), Djakarta, 1950, and Kahin, *Nationalism and Revolution,* pp. 122–27. The postindependence debates concerning the Pantjasila are recorded in the proceedings of the Constitutional Convention of 1956–57, *Tentang Dasar Negara Republik Indonesia Dalam Konstituante,* 3 vols. n.p. (probably Djakarta), n.d. (ca. 1958), perhaps the best example of ideological debate in a new nation so far available.

The "I am a follower of Karl Marx" quote is from Fisher,

The Story of Indonesia, p. 154; the statement about being simultaneously Christian, Muslim, and Hindu, ibid., p. 299; and the final quotation about Indonesia and the Almighty is from "Marhaen and Proletarian," p. 29.

On "Guided Democracy" and its expressions, see Fieth, "The Dynamics of Guided Democracy," in R. McVey, ed., *Indonesia* (New Haven, 1963), pp. 309–409.

Chapter 4

Pages 90–95

The best statement of B. Malinowski's position is his essay, "Magic, Science and Religion," most easily accessible in his *Magic, Science and Religion and Other Essays,* Chicago, 1948, from which the various quotations in my text are taken. Of Lévy-Bruhl's many works on "primitive thought," see, for a characteristic statement, *How Natives Think* (tr.), New York, 1926.

A. Schutz' ideas on the everyday world as the "paramount reality" in human experience are outlined in his *The Problem of Social Reality* (vol. 1 of his collected papers), The Hague, 1962.

Pages 95–116

Many of the ideas here discussed have been developed more systematically and in more detail in a number of my own writings over the past ten years, where appropriate, or anyway extensive, references can also be found: "Ethos, World View and the Analysis of Sacred Symbols," *The Antioch Review, 58* (1958), 421–37; "The Growth of Culture and the Evolution of Mind," in J. Scher, ed., *Theories of the Mind* (New York, 1962), pp. 713–40; "Ideology as a Cultural System," in D. Apter, ed., *Ideology and Discontent* (New York, 1964), pp. 47–76; "Religion as a Cultural System," in M. Banton, ed., *Anthropological Approaches to the Study of Religion* (London, 1966), pp. 204–15; *The Social History of an Indonesian Town* (Cambridge, Mass., 1965), pp. 119–208; *Person, Time and Conduct in Bali,* New Haven,

1966; "The Impact of the Concept of Culture on the Concept of Man," in J. Platt, ed., *New Views of the Nature of Man*, Chicago, 1966.

The reference to Alisdair MacIntyre on p. 98 is to his "The Logical Status of Religious Belief," in MacIntyre, ed., *Metaphysical Beliefs* (London, 1957), pp. 167–211.

The quotations from Abduh on p. 106 are from Cragg, *Counsels in Islam*, pp. 38, 39. Cragg's own aphorism is to be found in ibid., p. 37. For an interesting contemporary statement of the scripturalist position vis-à-vis science and secularism, which characterizes the two "strategies" outlined in the text as the "one-book" and the "two-book" approaches (and opts vigorously for the latter), see I. R. Al-Faruqi, "Science and Traditional Values in Islamic Society," *Zygon*, 2 (1967), pp. 231–46.

Index